Creating a Learning Society:
Initiatives for Education and Technology

A Report of
The Aspen Institute
Forum on Communications and Society

Amy Korzick Garmer
and
Charles M. Firestone
Rapporteurs

The
Aspen
Institute

Communications and Society Program
Charles M. Firestone
Director
Washington, DC
1996

For additional copies of this paper, please contact:

The Aspen Institute
Publications Office
109 Houghton Lab Lane
P.O. Box 222
Queenstown, MD 21658
Phone: (410) 820-5326
Fax: (410) 827-9174
E-mail: publications@aspeninst.org

For all other inquiries, please contact:

The Aspen Institute
Communications and Society Program
Suite 1070
1333 New Hampshire Avenue, NW
Washington, DC 20036
Phone: (202) 736-5818
Fax: (202) 467-0790

Contents

Preface

There is an unprecedented level of public concern about the state of education in America. This concern, driven by a variety of forces, includes increases in the cost to educate each student, the gap between skills and knowledge demanded by the modern workplace and the skills and knowledge graduating students possess, reliance on the school as a catch-all for social programs, and the numbers of students coming to school without the necessary readiness or supports to learn effectively. Increasingly, education is becoming an issue of "haves" and "have nots," and the impact of this widening gap is felt by all.

Reforming education to meet the needs of a rapidly changing world is a major undertaking that requires the redefinition of education and the whole system in which learning takes place. It requires innovative programs that explore new ways of approaching problems and solutions. It also requires greater appreciation for the many environments in which teaching and learning can occur, and the different ways in which individuals learn. The framework for change requires the effective collaboration of individuals and organizations in government, business, foundations, the nonprofit sector, communities, and educational institutions.

At the same time America faces the challenge of reforming its educational system, the communications revolution is making it possible to access greater quantities of information, faster and more efficiently than ever before. Technology is challenging the boundaries of the educational structures that have traditionally facilitated learning, from the schoolroom as the place where learning occurs, to the time limits of the school day and school year, and the role of the teacher as unique source of expertise. In this context, can the communications revolution play a positive role in meeting the educational goals of the country?

Forum on Communications and Society

In 1994, The Aspen Institute's Communications and Society Program created a forum for addressing the societal impact of the international information infrastructure at the highest levels of decision making. The Forum on Communications and Society (FOCAS) is a group of chief executives or their equivalents from business, government, and the nonprofit sector who meet annually to address different aspects of the societal impact of the communications and information infrastructure. The FOCAS suggests innovative ways that business, government, and the nonprofit sector might collaborate to use communications and information goods and services for the betterment of society. It does not attempt to duplicate existing activities, but rather to identify crucial issues where collaboration can make a difference to American society.

The Issue of Education

There is perhaps no issue at the intersection of technology and society more important or more immediately pressing than education. In its first two years, the FOCAS explored issues relating to the equitable and effective use of new technologies to enhance learning both inside and outside the classroom. Technology has the ability, figuratively speaking, to tear down the walls of the classroom, forcing people to recognize that learning is not an activity limited to the physical and administrative confines of the formal educational system. These implications naturally led the FOCAS from an emphasis on telecommunications and education in the K–12 classroom, in its first year, to learning and technology outside the classroom in its second. How will Americans acquire the skills needed to adapt to a rapidly changing world? What will happen if they don't? How do they ensure that their children are adequately prepared to enter this rapidly changing world?

The Role of Technology

New information and communications technologies are transforming the home and workplace by enhancing the discovery, access, and manipulation of information, and by increasing inter-action with others around the world. For the same reason, there is pressure on schools to transform the learning process by effective use of these same technologies. If used well, educational technology can be a powerful tool for improving the motivations and incentives for learning. It can also be an invaluable aid to teachers, revolutionizing the way that they practice their profession. While technology is not a panacea for the serious problems affecting education today, it can play an important role in preparing Americans of all ages for the future.

Educators, politicians, community activists, and representatives of American business all share a vision of an educational system that produces students with basic competencies in academic disciplines, higher order problem solving skills, and the functional literacies needed for the workforce of tomorrow. More importantly, our educational system must motivate students and create incentives for them to want to be lifelong learners. Creative uses of the new communications technologies, i.e., broadcast and cable television, video cassette recorders, computers, CD-ROM, electronic mail, the Internet, multimedia applications, and new wireless technologies, can offer students new opportunities to end the isolation of the classroom and discover useful information about people, places, and ideas. These technologies have the potential to engage people and instill a new excitement about learning.

Members of the FOCAS believe that individuals, businesses, governments, and the nonprofit sector share the responsibility of ensuring access to quality learning opportunities for every child in America, and to continuing learning opportunities for adults throughout their lives. To this end, the FOCAS has identified the following meaningful contributions to the problems of learning and technology, with particular emphasis on technology in the classroom. Briefly, the goals of the FOCAS in this area are:

- to improve the incentives for learning inside and outside the classroom;

- to promote equity and access in the acquisition and use of these technologies, and informed dialogue about the importance and benefits of learning technologies;

- to identify new sources of funds for technology in schools and communities;

- to assist educators in understanding and using the new tools for learning that technology offers; and

- to enhance learning opportunities for people of all ages and backgrounds through the use of communications and information technologies;

The following is a report on the underlying thinking and specific initiatives which the FOCAS has developed to address the goals stated above. Particularly, it sets forth some of the areas where public-private collaboration might make a difference. This report, however, does not imply the assent of any particular FOCAS entity to any particular statement. Rather, it is a reflection of the activity of the FOCAS and its follow-up task forces.

Much progress has been made since FOCAS members first met to discuss these issues, but there is still a long way to go before the educational system adapts to the new initiatives and new styles of learning in a technology driven age. FOCAS members are hopeful that this report can provide some useful ideas on how to move toward our goals, and that it encourages others to become involved in the process of transforming education in America.

Acknowledgments

We would like to gratefully acknowledge the members of the Forum on Communications and Society for their commitment to this project and the time they have dedicated to grappling with these very important issues of learning and technology. Members of the FOCAS in its first two years are listed below. Special thanks go to R. Bruce Bradley, President and Publisher of the *Virginian Pilot*, Alexander Kroll, CEO Emeritus of Young & Rubicam, and P. Michael Timpane, President Emeritus of Teachers College at Columbia University and Vice President and Senior Scholar at the Carnegie Foundation for the Advancement of Teaching, for their expert participation in the 1995 FOCAS meeting. We also wish to acknowledge the work of the participants in the FOCAS Summer

Preparatory sessions, the Task Force meetings following up on the FOCAS initiatives, and the resource people whom we have enlisted in this effort. The list of these participants appears in the Appendix. In particular, Dr. Linda Roberts has given enthusiastic support to our efforts since the beginning and has been an invaluable resource for the project. We also want to acknowledge our consultants in 1994 and 1995, Dr. Barbara Kurshan and Dr. Arthur Sheekey, respectively; Katherine Harting Travers, our rapporteur in 1995; Christopher Welton, our Amherst College summer intern, who researched the school funding proposals described in this report; and all the others who have provided guidance and expert advice to us in the preparation of this report.

Amy Korzick Garmer   Charles M. Firestone
Senior Program Associate   Director

Communications and Society Program
The Aspen Institute

MEMBERS OF THE FORUM ON COMMUNICATIONS AND SOCIETY, 1994–95

James Barr, III
President and CEO
TDS Telecommunications Corp.

Edward A. Bennett
Chief Executive Officer
Prodigy Services

David Britt
President and CEO
Children's Television Workshop

Ronald H. Brown
Secretary
U.S. Department of Commerce

Gaston Caperton
Governor, West Virginia

Elaine Chao
President and CEO
United Way of America

Ramon Cortines
Former Chancellor
New York City Public Schools

Rudolph Crew
Chancellor
New York City Public Schools

Joseph L. Dionne
Chairman, President and CEO
McGraw-Hill, Inc.

Ervin Duggan
Chairman and CEO
Public Broadcasting Service

Joan M. Dykstra
President
The National PTA

Ross Glatzer
Former Chief Executive Officer
Prodigy Services

Susan Golding
Mayor
San Diego, California

William H. Gray, III
President and CEO
United Negro College Fund

John Hendricks
Chairman and CEO
Discovery Communications, Inc.

Jim Hirshfield
President and CEO
Summit Communications

Stanley Hubbard
Chief Executive Officer
Hubbard Broadcasting

Reed Hundt
Chairman
Federal Communications
    Commission

Glenn Jones
Chairman and CEO
Jones Intercable

Robert Kerrey
United States Senator

Gerald Levin
Chairman and CEO
Time Warner Inc.

Delano Lewis
President and CEO
National Public Radio

Edward Lupberger
Chairman and CEO
Entergy Corporation

Russell Mawby
Former Chairman and CEO
W. K. Kellogg Foundation

Richard McCormick
President and CEO
US West, Inc.

David McLaughlin
President and CEO
The Aspen Institute

Jean Monty
President and CEO
Northern Telecom Limited

Lloyd Morrisett
President
The John and Mary R. Markle
    Foundation

Albin Moschner
Chairman and CEO
Zenith Electronics Corporation

Richard Notebaert
President and CEO
Ameritech

Jerry Pearlman
Former Chairman and CEO
Zenith Electronics Corporation

Hugh Price
President
The National Urban League

William Richardson
Chairman and CEO
W. K. Kellogg Foundation

Albert Shanker
President
American Federation of Teachers

Kathryn Whitfill
Former President
The National PTA

John Wynne
Chief Executive Officer
Landmark Communications, Inc.

Raul Yzaguirre
President
National Council of La Raza

Creating a Learning Society: Initiatives for Education and Technology

PART ONE:
LEARNING AND TECHNOLOGY

When the FOCAS first met, members found it useful to make a distinction between education and learning. Education, the members thought, connotes an institutionalized system that carries with it a considerable amount of political baggage in the wake of controversies over the performance and control of American public schools. Learning, on the other hand, invokes a very human process that lies beyond the control of any particular party or constituency. Thus, when the FOCAS embarked on its examination of how communications and information technologies might be employed for the benefit of society, *learning* became the central concept of the discussion. This distinction was useful because it placed the individual learner, rather than the class, school or educational system, at the heart of the discussion and enabled the group to focus on the interaction between the individual and the technology.

A year later, when the FOCAS convened to examine issues of technology and learning outside the classroom, members reconsidered the validity of making a rigid distinction between the two terms. After all, they reasoned, learning is a process and a habit that ought to be encouraged throughout a lifetime. But before one can have lifelong learning, there has to be something to build on. That something is childhood learning. And for better or worse, childhood learning is greatly dependent on the six hours per day that most children spend in school. Moreover, the skills and knowledge needed to succeed in the workplace and those needed

1

to succeed in college are becoming more and more the same. Ideally, the experiences of students in the formal educational system should be a significant part of the continuum of learning that spans across a lifetime.

Still, FOCAS members found that the problems of integrating technology into schools and into learning outside the classroom raise two distinct sets of issues. The two issues, dubbed "wiring the children" and "lifelong learning," are related, but the former is perhaps better developed as a notion of the latter, and society does not accept the two with equal enthusiasm. "The issue of technology in the classrooms is a highly organized, ongoing debate," said Michael Timpane, President Emeritus of Columbia Teachers College and Senior Scholar at the Carnegie Endowment for the Advancement of Teaching, "whereas the idea of a learning society is one where we are feeling our way."

This report reflects the struggle to make sense of these two issues as part of a larger whole. The first section briefly describes the changes in the paradigm of learning that are driven by new communications and information technologies, and outlines the principles of equity and access on which the FOCAS believes the use of technology ought to be based. This section then describes how new technologies can impact learning, particularly in the classroom, and sets forth the barriers within the educational system that hinder the adoption and effective use of technology. Section two then looks at the most significant barriers to technology in the classroom, funding and teacher training, and presents a variety of initiatives that the FOCAS believes can make a difference in overcoming these obstacles and in promoting greater public awareness of technologies for learning. Finally, section three addresses the issue of using technology for learning outside the classroom and the challenge of creating a society of lifelong learners.

A Changing Paradigm for Learning

Our understanding of the many ways in which people learn has expanded significantly over the past several decades. Moreover, there is a greater appreciation for the myriad environments in which learning can take place and the importance of context to the learning process. Learning can occur in many different settings, inside and outside of the classroom, and at any time. It can be passively experienced, consciously sought, or entirely serendipitous. This report understands learning to be an essentially human process that takes place throughout a lifetime.

New communications and information technologies are driving dramatic changes in learning. As a result, the paradigm for learning is shifting away from the traditional notion that "knowledge" is transferred from teacher to student within the confines of the classroom, and that mastery of a body of knowledge over the course of sixteen or more years is the goal. Instead, a new understanding of learning places the learner at the center of the learning process, with the teacher serving an important supporting role in facilitating the process. In the new paradigm, successful learning is certified by an individual's ability to apply the appropriate tools and information to the solution of problems encountered throughout a lifetime.

A challenge inheres in this new concept of learning. It is the necessity to *unlearn* old habits and notions of how learning should be structured, and instead to develop new habits of instruction that motivate learners to take greater control over their own education, from preschool through adulthood. Understanding learners' motivations and goals is the first step on this path to expanding opportunities for learning. In the view of FOCAS members, the primary goals for learning include *personal goals*, such as self-improvement, developing a greater sense of self control, and spiritual fulfillment; *economic goals*, such as gaining marketable skills and knowledge that enable individuals to support themselves and their families; and *social goals* that lead to greater civic participation and engagement.

For individuals, the new structure of learning requires greater personal responsibility and autonomy that many people may not be comfortable or prepared to assume. Likewise, teachers will have to give up a measure of control over the learning process and adapt to a new position on the sidelines as educational "coaches." For businesses, government, and the nonprofit sector, the new structure of learning must ensure equitable access to the resources necessary for learners to participate fully in society.

The Challenge of Universal Access

If America is going to sustain a high standard of living, remain globally competitive, and maintain a healthy civic culture into the 21st century, it must invite all its citizens to participate in and share continuous learning experiences—in schools, at home, in the workplace, and through community institutions. The nation's social and economic conditions are being transformed, and there is justification to rethink how education and opportunities for learning are extended to all citizens. But as the current debate over the state of American education suggests, there are grave doubts about how well we are doing in this regard.

"We are suffering a failure of the ethic of access," said Ervin Duggan, president of the Public Broadcasting Service. "We are underperforming compared to previous efforts." Indeed, America has a long tradition of innovation in education and expanding access to learning opportunities to all its citizens. In the 18th century, the idea of free public education was championed by Thomas Jefferson, among others, in the face of criticism that it would bankrupt the nascent republic. Arguably, as Duggan pointed out, "it was a great feat of social imagination" that opened up previously unattainable opportunities for millions of people. This was followed in the 19th century by the creation of the land grant colleges, which extended access to affordable, advanced education beyond the limitations of the primary school system.

With the technological progress of the 20th century, attention turned to broadcasting, and in the 1950s visionaries in the federal government set aside broadcasting spectrum for educational uses. The spectrum set aside for educational use has enabled individuals and communities isolated by geographic, economic, and other barriers to access quality educational programming, often at little or no cost, through public broadcasting, cable television programming such as Jones Intercable's Mind Extension University (ME/U), distance learning programs, and other systems.

In spite of this tradition of universal access to education, the gap between those who succeed as learners and those who are left behind is widening. Jonathan Kozol called attention to this fact in his 1991 book, *Savage Inequalities*, and the evidence in the intervening years does not suggest that the situation has improved. FOCAS members recognize this widening gap as the greatest cause for concern over education today. Echoing Kozol, Timpane noted, "The disgrace of our nation is that we tolerate the amount of inequality and dispersion of quality in our public schools. No other of our competitors tolerates the amount of inequality. No other nation can make the claim to have some of the best schools in the world and some of the worst schools in the world. That's the problem."

As we prepare for the 21st century, new communications and information technologies offer the possibility of expanding access to opportunities for learning. Getting technological tools and information into the hands of every student, and ensuring that they are put to beneficial use, are the challenges facing America today. "Leadership at the state level is critical, and particularly important with technology," noted Linda Roberts, Director of the Office of Educational Technology at the U.S. Department of Education and chief technology advisor to Secretary of Education Richard Riley. Equally important is the involvement of parents, businesses, and other members of the community. "But we have to be very clear about where we want to go," Roberts cautioned. It is clear that progress in education will not come without certain costs, which will have to be weighed against the cost of doing nothing.

The Potential of Technology for Education

For centuries, teachers have used chalk and books to aid in teaching. The revolutions in computers and communications technology have given teachers and students an immense array of tools to enhance learning. Broadcast and cable television, the VCR, computers, the Internet, CD-ROM, electronic mail, multimedia applications, and new wireless technologies—all of these offer the possibility of discovering new and exciting information about people, places, and ideas. The creative use of these technologies has the potential to engage young people and instill an excitement about learning in ways that few traditional teaching aids and techniques seem capable of doing.

These technologies can engage students in discovery through simulation and exploration of new concepts, connect them to people and ideas beyond the classroom, and expand educational content beyond what was formerly available. Technologies can aid teachers in adapting materials to different learning styles and promote equity in education by providing a diverse range of resources and experiences to students who might not otherwise be able to afford them. They can facilitate administrative tasks and communication with parents, and enhance professional development. They have been linked to increased self-motivation of individual learners and can promote collaborative learning among students. Ultimately, technology in the classroom can contribute to individual readiness for the technology-rich workplace of the future.

What Technology Can Do to Enhance Learning

- enhance discovery through simulation and exploration of new concepts
- connect individuals to new people and ideas and expand content beyond what was previously available
- promote equity by providing a diverse array of resources and experiences to those who might not otherwise be able to afford them
- adapt to and accommodate different learning styles through modularized, self-paced, just-in-time learning and nonthreatening learning environments
- increase self-motivation of learners
- promote collaborative learning
- promote readiness for the technology-rich workplace of the future
- improve learning productivity by delivering more opportunities for learning to more people at potentially lower cost
- overcome time and distance barriers
- promote value of individual creation & distribution by permitting people to share their own learning process and results with others
- enhance professional development
- facilitate communication among teachers, learners, and parents
- facilitate administrative tasks
- create channels for people to participate more easily in local and national public policy, debates, and action

Gaston Caperton, Governor of West Virginia, described how his state's test scores have soared since the progressive implementation of technology in public schools. "We used to fight with Mississippi for last place, but now we're 19th overall in the nationwide rankings for reading, writing, math, and computer skills. Mississippi says they miss us!" he quipped. David Britt, President of Children's Television Workshop, is another witness to the phenomenon. "Interactivity leads to fundamental changes in the ways people use learning. The power of interactivity is a quantum jump," Britt said. "And it's easy," Caperton added. "Four computers and some training will change the way a class learns."

While generally enthusiastic about the potential of technology to enhance learning, FOCAS members did not ignore the downside to technology that is ill-applied or not equitably distributed. Raul Yzaguirre, President of the National Council of La Raza, initiated this discussion with his observation that technology represents both a promise and a threat—a promise of helping to achieve the goals we are seeking in education, and a threat in that technology can also widen the gap between information haves and have nots. The duality that inheres in this way of looking at technology is useful and worth mentioning, especially with regard to the widening gap between rich and poor.

Furthermore, "a wired society may not be a civil society," Yzaguirre continued. "It may atrophy our social skills, erode our affinities and sense of community, and contribute to a 'modem on the mountain top' mentality." He offered these cautionary notes while acknowledging the evident benefits of technology to his constituency: "Hispanic children are now the largest minority in public schools, but they are undereducated and the gap is widening. The issues are testing and tracking. ESL [English as a Second Language] kids do poorly on tests and are put in slow tracks. We want education to be a more individuated experience, and technology enables that." He summed up by saying, "It's wrong to say that technology is a dangerous force, but it's equally wrong to say there are no dangers."

Technology, if implemented well, can be a powerful tool for improving the motivations and incentives for learning and access to quality educational opportunities. It can also be an invaluable aid to teachers, revolutionizing the way that they practice their profession, and involving parents more directly in their children's learning. While technology is not a panacea for the serious problems affecting education today, it can play an important role in preparing America's children for the future.

States and school administrators have recognized the positive impact that technology can have on learning and are making efforts to connect schools. There are now 5.8 million computers in American schools, or about one for every nine students, and 75 percent of schools have access to some kind of computer network. There are at least one television set and one VCR per school. But while the investments in and acquisition of hardware have increased in recent years, investments in technology support, software, and curriculum development, and most importantly, teacher training, have lagged far behind. These are critical components of achieving equitable access to technology.

It is worth noting that there is a distinction to be made between *equal* access to technology and *equitable* access. *Equal* access suggests that there are equal numbers of computers, VCRs, and other technology elements in schools, and that schools receive an equal amount of funding for technology (which is frequently distributed on a per-pupil basis). Equal access focuses on the quantity available. *Equitable* access is a qualitative assessment which focuses on variables beyond the sheer number of technology elements. These variables include creating a physical environment that is conducive to learning, the technological aptitude of teachers using the technology, general information literacy, parental involvement, and other factors that affect the ability of students to learn effectively with technology.

Technology Needs of American Schools

All of America's children deserve an education that will prepare them to become active learners and productive citizens throughout their lives. Children should come to school motivated and ready to learn, regardless of their backgrounds, and they should have available all the technological tools for learning that society can provide.

But America's schools need more than just pipelines bringing information into the classroom. They need tools for teachers in the classroom, such as computers, telephones, and electronic mail connections to parents and students in the home. They need data and communications connections to community-based networks and the Internet, and access to high quality software and applications that can be integrated into the school curriculum. They need teachers who are trained to use these technological tools and sufficient support to maintain the technology so that these tools can be used effectively in the classroom and beyond. Ultimately, classrooms should be information rich through data communication and video resources from the community and all over the world. Interactive technologies should be used to end the isolation of the classroom.

How well is society meeting these needs? Current statistics tell part of the story:

- The United States spends approximately $275 billion per year for kindergarten through high school education. Of this amount, $2.4 billion was spent on educational technology in 1994, according to the Software Publishers Association.

- There is, on average, one computer for every nine students in U.S. schools. Many of these computers, however, are older models that do not have the power to perform more advanced functions such as those involving video and the Internet.

- The Department of Education reports that even though a majority of public schools have access to some kind of computer network, and 50 percent have access to the Internet, only 9 percent of all instructional classrooms in public schools are connected to the Internet. Furthermore, in those schools with Internet access, information services are more often available to teachers and administrative staff than to students. The greatest access is in secondary schools and in schools of 1,000 or more students.

- The most widely available Internet capability is e-mail, which is available to 90 percent of schools with Internet access. Graphical user interfaces, such as Netscape, are available to only 21 percent of schools with Internet access.

- Sixty percent of schools in central cities report having insufficient information technology elements, compared with 52 percent in suburbs and 46 percent in rural towns, according to a 1995 study by the General Accounting Office. Schools with predominately minority populations report insufficient technology in greater percentages than schools with fewer minority students.

While the trends are moving in the right direction, it is still appropriate to ask whether America's students are able to keep pace with the rapid technological changes taking place in society. Of particular concern is the question of equity. Statistics also show that students from particular racial, ethnic, and geographical backgrounds are less likely to have technology available to foster improved learning opportunities than their wealthier counterparts. Due to a variety of barriers, some of America's students are being left behind.

Barriers to Equitable Access

There are many barriers that inhibit the widespread use of the new learning technologies. Perhaps the most talked about are the funding barriers, although as more schools gain connections to these technologies, the other barriers—structural, technological, attitudinal, and navigational—are becoming more significant. Some schools face more of these barriers than others. While the following is not intended to be an exhaustive list, it does summarize many of the significant hurdles to be overcome.

Financial Barriers
According to the Department of Education, financial barriers are most often cited as limits to the acquisition and use of advanced telecommunications technologies. The costs of hardware, training, support, software, and services, and retrofitting older facilities to accommodate the new technologies, create a formidable barrier to equitable access to telecommunications technologies. These prob-

lems are compounded by the lack of experience that schools bring to planning, budgeting, and purchasing technology and related services, and the lack of adequate training and educational software once the hardware has been purchased. A lack of equitable sourcing of funds contributes to the difficulties that students in particularly disadvantaged areas have in accessing learning technologies. That is, the wide array of funding sources available to schools in wealthier areas often contributes to a widening gap between haves and have-nots.

Technological Barriers

Closely related to the funding barriers are technological barriers, which include lack of the necessary technical infrastructure and expertise to support the new communications and information technologies. Technological barriers include insufficient electrical outlets in a classroom to support multiple pieces of equipment, limited telephone lines to the school, and insufficient technical support once the equipment is in place.

Structural Barriers

The traditional organizational structure of schools constitutes another set of barriers that can be referred to as structural barriers. The hierarchical structure of American school systems has tended to hinder communication between teachers and school administrators. This lack of communication means that administrators responsible for purchasing and planning for technology often do not receive adequate input from the individuals most affected by the technology, the teachers who use it in the classroom.

The rigidity with which traditional academic disciplines have been taught, with a bias against interdisciplinary approaches, presents an additional structural barrier to the introduction of technology. Some of the most effective uses of Internet resources, for example, are in their application to complex problems that cross traditional subject boundaries. Additionally, traditional methods of student assessment, especially the reliance on standardized tests, inhibit teachers from experimenting with technological tools. The ability to manage information resources and discovery techniques that students develop through technology-aided simulation and exploration are not effectively evaluated through normal testing mechanisms, which are used to measure both student and teacher performance.

Attitudinal Barriers

These structural barriers exacerbate the psychological or attitudinal barriers that accompany the introduction of technology into a new environment. Many teachers and administrators are entrenched in the old paradigm of education, in which the teacher lectures to rows of students seated at their desks with pencils poised to take notes in their notebooks. Many are not yet ready to relinquish some measure of control over student learning to the students themselves.

Unlearning old habits is perhaps easier said than done, especially given the teacher-centered design and conservative nature of the nation's educational system. "The formal education system is still coming to grips with how to change its thinking and how to bring about a learning society rather than how to run educational institutions," said Timpane. He adds, "Teaching is fine, but learning is more important. Educators thought they had a corner on learning, but technology is changing that."

These attitudes may be grounded in a general discomfort with or fear of technology. After all, children often know more about computers and video recorders than their teachers. Such reluctance may also be fueled by a lack of compelling reasons, incentives, or rewards for incorporating technology into the curriculum, and is compounded by a lack of support from educational administrators and parents.

Content and Navigational Barriers

Content and navigational barriers present a final hurdle to equitable access to learning technologies. The materials a teacher or student needs may not exist. Alternatively, the materials may, in fact, exist, but the teacher or student does not know what is available or how to access the materials. This is essentially a training problem. And, finally, school officials are increasingly citing the availability of inappropriate materials on the information superhighway as a reason for delaying connection to the Internet.

The Need for Collaboration

Partnerships and cross-sectoral collaborations can vastly improve learning opportunities for America's children. Leaders in the public and private sectors can promote learning opportunities for all students by:

- speaking in support of equitable access to the new tools for learning when they have the opportunity to do so;

- seeking opportunities to get involved in partnerships with schools and other members of the community;

- developing creative funding strategies that might break down the barriers to acquiring and using technology effectively;

- creating materials and support networks for teachers and administrators interested in learning more about the new technologies and how they can enhance teaching and learning; and

- educating the public about the benefits of integrating technology into the classroom through public service campaigns and public forums on education and technology.

The following section represents the work of the FOCAS and its follow-up task forces. Rather than simply talk about the problems of education and technology, FOCAS members are interested in seeking solutions. Their desire to develop creative solutions to the most pressing barriers to accessing technology for learning— funding the technology, teacher training, and public support for technology in the classroom—has resulted in the following initiatives that envision informed dialogue and cross-sectoral collaborations as necessary components in expanding access to learning, on an equitable basis, to the next generation of Americans.

PART TWO:
PROMOTING EQUITABLE ACCESS
TO TECHNOLOGY
IN THE CLASSROOM

The FOCAS believes that the most effective way of creating incentives to overcome the barriers to the use of technology in the classroom is to build partnerships among various members of the community. Business people, community leaders, teachers, administrators, parents, students, and representatives from all levels of government, higher education, and the media have important roles to play in preparing students for the future, and all have a stake in the outcome. All can help to meet the technology-related needs of the classroom.

There is a need to support the funding of technology and related services in new and creative ways, especially if all students are to receive the benefits of the information superhighway. In many state funding formulas, the focus is on equalizing the amount of money spent per pupil. Meanwhile, little is being done to equalize the capital side of the equation that affects the ability to access technology. Different aspects of technology should be funded in different ways, so that software and teacher training funds do not necessarily come out of the same budget as hardware and facilities upgrades. Schools should be allowed to make money from the technology they have, for example, by opening up media centers beyond normal school hours to the community for a nominal fee. Additionally, experienced nonprofit and other organizations could offer assistance with writing proposals so that schools can compete for some of the grant money available for community-based technology projects.

There is a need to support teachers and administrators in their use of technology for learning. With the constraints of their daily schedules, teachers have little time in which to pursue opportunities for professional development and to learn about the new tools that technologies offer. In most districts, professional development is limited to a handful of designated days throughout the school year. But learning to integrate technology into the classroom so that it becomes a seamless tool takes time and practice, and requires a significant amount of support from administrators and parents. Add to the equation the extra demands for social services that schools in disadvantaged and low income areas place on teachers, and it is no wonder that some teachers have been slow to adopt technology.

There is a need, then, for more and better opportunities for teachers to learn about communications and information technologies and how to use them, and for new incentives for teachers to experiment with technology in the classroom. Furthermore, school districts need to recruit a core group of excellent teachers in each state who can set the standard for using the new technologies in the classroom.

So far, educators have done a poor job of making the case for businesses' involvement in education. And until recently, too few businesses have stepped forward to offer assistance where they could make a difference, particularly in dealing with the tough issues of planning, budgeting, funding, and training. The recent "NetDay" project in California, in which volunteers from technology companies and other organizations spread out across the state on March 9, 1996, to wire as many schools as possible, captures the spirit of collaboration that is desperately needed. The education summit convened in March 1996 at IBM headquarters in New York, which was attended by at least one FOCAS member, may serve as an additional catalyst for businesses' involvement in education. Collaborations between higher education and K–12 teachers could also spur curricular development and begin to address some of the issues involved in training teachers and identifying the most beneficial applications for student learning.

Critical Issues of Funding

Funding is the major barrier most often cited in the acquisition or use of advanced telecommunications in public schools. According to a recent Department of Education report, schools cited funding as a major barrier 69 percent of the time, ranking this factor first in a list of potential barriers. Other major barriers most often cited were lack of equipment or poor equipment (50 percent) and too few access points in the school building (47 percent).[1]

There are five major cost areas associated with the implementation of technology in schools: hardware, retrofitting of older school facilities to accommodate the new telecommunications infrastructure, training, software and services, and support.[2] School administrators must look beyond funding hardware only (which has been the focus until recently), and place equal or greater emphasis on training, support, and the development of useful and effective content and software applications for education.

Creating incentives, rather than imposing mandates, is by far the most preferred method for funding educational technology. The purchase of equipment makes no sense if educators have no interest in using the technology. Incentives would create demand for greater use of technologies in the learning process, provide an impetus for further experimentation and innovation, and, if applied appropriately, improve both the opportunities for learning and the outcomes. Schools should be encouraged to contribute content, and rewarded for their contributions. This could, in turn, generate additional funds to be applied toward educational technology and related services. Finally, in addressing the issues relating to funding of learning technologies, issues of planning and budgeting are critical to the successful adoption of technology.

Criteria

In developing new strategies for funding educational technology, the following criteria should be considered: *Is the proposal politically viable? Is the proposal economically feasible and significant? Is it scalable? Is the proposal (or combination of proposals) a positive gain for all parties involved? That is, can all parties see tangible benefits which meet or exceed their outlays?*

Proposals

The following proposals are distilled from a series of task force meetings and other follow-up activity aimed at determining whether there are new and creative means of funding the classroom connections discussed above. This area is most difficult, of course, as it involves the actual spending of money in an environment of increasing costs and demands, yet fewer revenues are available to the schools. Nevertheless, the promise of significant returns on investment, in terms of increased learning skills and preparation for the world of tomorrow, warrant continued attention, creativity, and scrutiny. We are hopeful that at least some of the approaches to funding described in this report may find success in various school districts around the country.

Networking the Classroom

There are five distinct funding items necessary for the creation of a functional and beneficial network connection to the classroom. These are:

- *School Connection:* The purchase of terminal equipment, such as computers, CD-ROM drives, televisions, video cassette players, telephones (collectively, "hardware"), and physical connections between schools and the rest of the network.

- *Classroom Connection:* Hardware purchases and physical connections between the school's network connection and classrooms within the school. Generally this means funding inside wiring and/or a local area network (LAN) of some sort.

- *Support and Maintenance:* Adequate staffing and technical support to maintain equipment and connections once they are in place and to upgrade equipment over time.

- *Teacher Training:* Thorough training of teachers to work with the hardware, select appropriate software and applications, and effectively integrate them into the curriculum. The type of professional development envisioned for teacher training is a continual process, requiring the additional resources of time and expert personnel.

- *Data Transmission:* Affordable data transmission rates for network access.

A sixth item, appropriate, affordable, and updated software and other curriculum materials, was recognized as being very important to the successful integration of technology into the learning process. However, this item was not discussed in great detail by the FOCAS, and so does not appear in the list of funding initiatives below. It was clear that funds will need to be allocated to develop appropriate materials. Educational software companies and other entrepreneurs will be responsible for developing some of these materials. Where the appropriate materials cannot be purchased off the shelf, however, some of the funding mechanisms outlined below may prove useful in putting money into the hands of educational professionals for this important purpose.

While many communities are making strides toward alleviating the funding problem, the financial plight of governments at all levels requires that new and innovative solutions arise from business and community collaborations. The following suggests a number of innovative ways that school districts, governments, businesses, and communities might work together to fund the effective use of communications and information technologies in the classroom.

School Connection

Because it is basically a one-time investment, school connection is perhaps the most straightforward network funding cost. There are four approaches to funding such connections: school or private entrepreneurship, telecommunications company cross-subsidization, direct government financing, and government guarantees.

PRIVATE ENTREPRENEURSHIP. At least one entrepreneurial company is packaging the costs of wiring to and within the schools, the equipment, and teacher training, and amortizing these costs to the school district through a per-student charge over a three year time span. This enables the company to expend the capital to purchase the goods initially, and the school district to operationalize the costs over a reasonable time period, all within the normal, but creative use of market mechanisms.

TELECOMMUNICATIONS COMPANY CROSS-SUBSIDIZATION. Several companies, some of them FOCAS members, are voluntarily wiring the schools within their franchise areas without cost to the schools. Indeed, at least in part as a result of initial contacts at the FOCAS meeting in 1994, the FCC proposed a "social contract" with Time

Warner Cable in 1995 to wire schools within the company's franchise area free of charge and to wire classrooms at cost.[3] FOCAS members, such as Ameritech, and many other telephone and cable companies have already connected schools in their franchise areas—all through internal cross-subsidizations. We have appended to this report a summary, prepared in connection with another Aspen Institute Communications and Society project, which details some of the efforts of the telecommunications, cable, and other industries to effect greater diffusion of technology for classroom learning.

While these are two useful approaches, they are quite limited in application. There is still a strong need for other creative ways to finance the cost of school and classroom connections.

GOVERNMENT FINANCING. Some have proposed that the school connection be financed directly from revenues which the Federal Communications Commission is reaping from a variety of spectrum auctions. There is a certain logic to this, as it would redirect revenues from the communications industry into socially beneficial uses of the communications infrastructure. Because this proposal has been advocated by Vice President Al Gore, among others, but has not been adopted by Congress, we do not belabor it here, except in the following scenario where funds could be used instead as back up guarantees for an agency that would secure loans to finance the connections (see below).

GOVERNMENT GUARANTEES FOR A LENDING AUTHORITY. A more creative approach proposed by the McGuffey Project[4] is to establish a national authority to secure bonds and loans—similar in nature to the Federal National Mortgage Association (Fannie Mae) or the Federal Home Loan Mortgage Corporation (Freddie Mac) in the home mortgage market. Once capitalized, the authority could reduce bond underwriting costs to school districts by re-ducing the risk of bond or loan default, thus lowering loan interest rates and increasing investor confidence in bonds. In the loan market, medium and long term loans would be issued at reduced interest rates. Under the McGuffey Project approach, this scheme would be applicable only for initial network connections. The lending authority would exist only until such time as every school in America was connected to the national switched network.

To capitalize the lending authority, the McGuffey Project recommends that any actual FCC spectrum auction proceeds exceeding the expected auction amount be used. There are two advantages to this approach, as opposed to using the auction proceeds to wire the classrooms directly. First, the auction proceeds needed to capitalize a lending authority are significantly less than what would be needed to pay for a direct grant program. Second, the federal government would simply give up access to the auction proceeds for the limited duration of the program. After near-universal school connection is achieved, the authority's capital would revert to the Federal Treasury where it could be used for deficit reduction or other purposes. In this manner, the federal government could still take an active role in developing school network connections while not making any new expenditures from general revenue.

To address the issue of equity, particularly in traditionally under-served and under-financed school districts, an additional "safety net" program composed of unified federal grants could be directed to those schools unable to raise the necessary monies in the open market. Or, the federal government could purchase bonds from schools qualifying for assistance. In this scheme, assistance would be approved to provide a basic standard of service (which remains to be determined). Such a program would provide funds only to the poorest districts that meet geographic or average income requirements, and only after applicants have exhausted all other possible funding alternatives.

Classroom Connection

While school connection needs are relatively constant across the nation, classroom connection needs are highly dependent upon individual school buildings. For some schools, such as those with significant amounts of asbestos, retrofitting costs can dwarf networking costs. In others schools, local area networks (LANs) have already been installed. Also included in this category are the costs of acquiring terminals, computers, modems, and other hardware necessary to network one or more classrooms within the school building, and teachers and students within the classrooms. Local choice and multiple national vendors are generally available for LAN installation and equipment purchases.

GOVERNMENT FINANCING AND GUARANTEES OF SECURED LENDING. The funding approaches to school connections described above could also apply to classroom connections. Both involve the purchase of hardware equipment and the hard wiring of telecommunications to the schools in the first instance and inside the schools in the second. Ideally, where there are loan or bond applications involved, school connection and classroom connection funds would be a coupled investment, with schools required to present a comprehensive network deployment plan with their loan or bond application.

In addition, the following are offered as additional suggestions for funding the classroom connection, which is often more expensive than the initial school link.

DEPRECIATION DEDUCTIONS AND TAX CREDITS. This unique and innovative approach would establish depreciation schedules for each of the goods purchased by a school district. At present, since public and nonprofit schools do not pay taxes, normal depreciation of equipment does not benefit them financially. However, under this proposal, the depreciation deduction available to those who file tax returns would be alienable by school districts to vendors of the equipment, thereby lowering the cost and allowing schools to update their equipment.

The Internal Revenue Service would establish regulations whereby a school that purchases equipment for networking or otherwise advancing learning in the classroom would have available a depreciation schedule for such equipment. Certificates would be issued to vendors from whom the school purchased equipment, allowing them a deduction. To prevent unjust enrichment, the vendor would have to certify that it provided equipment to the school district at a discount. This would significantly lower the cost of equipment purchased by the schools.

Additionally, allowing telephone and cable companies to write-off the cost of providing infrastructure to schools over a one-to-five year period instead of over a longer period, such as 16 years, would provide an accelerated cash flow incentive to fund connection efforts.

VOUCHERS. To offer maximum flexibility to states and localities, a voucher system might be established to help fund hardware and network installations. That is, the schools would receive a certain amount of funds in the form of vouchers at the federal or state level with which to purchase network goods and services. Recipients could use these vouchers as tax credits on their tax returns at the federal or state level.

Vouchers could be issued on a sliding average income scale. The richest school districts would have the highest fund-to-voucher ratio, while the poorest districts would receive the majority of their money from tax vouchers with only a minimum school district contribution. Moreover, local school districts could be required to pay matching funds and to write a comprehensive technology integration plan to demonstrate their awareness of and commitment to technology in the classroom as part of the requirement for receiving vouchers.

The vouchers could be used for other networking needs as well. For example, vouchers applied to income tax and depreciation deductions for teachers purchasing educational technology would facilitate teacher familiarity with new technology. Vouchers might also be used for maintenance and support of communications systems and hardware.

Technology vouchers could be funded in a number of ways. Among the most reliable sources of funding would be an expanded universal service fund or taxes collected as general revenue or excise taxes.

UNIVERSAL SERVICE FUND. The universal service fund has traditionally been used to increase access to telephone service for residential, rural, and low-income users. The Telecommunications Act of 1996 expands the universal service fund to include schools as beneficiaries for the first time. It provides for a redefinition of universal service to include the principle that schools, health care providers, and libraries should have access to advanced telecommunications services, and directs the FCC and the states to determine how schools are to be included under the universal service system. The universal service fund, then, could be used to finance vouchers or other government subsidies for telecommunications services.[5]

TAXES. Technology vouchers could also be funded from general revenues. Such a voucher system for the purchase of educational technology (including software) could be established along the following principles: (1) Tax revenue is the most effec-tive public revenue source. (2) Revenue should come from those who benefit most. In principle, this means either general revenues or a special tax on those industries which profit from new technologies. (3) Incentives work better than mandates for stimulating investment.

Perhaps the most effective voucher funding method would be an excise tax on hardware and software. Some preliminary figures indicate that, at one percent per year, potential federal revenues could exceed $1 billion per year. A similar excise tax on telecommunications rates could yield an additional $1 billion annually.[6]

Vouchers funded by such an excise tax would be redeemable only within taxed industries. Thus, technology vouchers could not be used to pay for books or salaries. Depending upon available funding, however, a manufacturer's tax credit for educational software, to be funded by the excise tax, could be created. This would create an incentive/disincentive system for companies to direct a significant portion of their resources toward developing the educational market. One example of such a policy is Missouri's law that taxes video tape rentals.

SCHOOL ENTREPRENEURSHIP AND BUDGET REFORMS. School entrepreneurship and budget reforms are rather simple and desirable ways to help fund technology in the classroom. This includes reviewing the way that funds are currently allocated under education budgets, and considering new allocations of funds. For example, the State of Texas pioneered the practice of allowing textbook funds to be spent on software.

Incentives for income generated by schools from outside sources should be part of the budget process as well. As school boards explore funding for education from sources other than property taxes and state budget allocations, creative solutions abound. One state has linked its training costs for public safety officers and classrooms, using schools as the training sites. Forty percent of training costs is in travel, and the money saved by officers staying within their own communities for training is shared with schools to pay for distance learning classroom costs.

In one of the country's largest school districts, the school system is establishing a not-for-profit company to provide Internet access to the community. The district already has the necessary LANs in place to support community Internet access, and will now attempt to capitalize on investments already made. Revenues should continue to support technology in the schools. An added educational benefit is that students will be involved in all aspects of the service, learning about the technology as they help the broader community, and community residents can connect directly with the school system's telecommunications and content offerings.

Additional proposals for school-generated revenues include:

- Marketing programs with local businesses to apply credits for the sale of goods or services to the school's purchase of technology. One example is a bank that issues credit cards for which a 1 percent rebate on all purchases goes to local schools. A similar program was established by a long distance company in rural Illinois that set up an "Earning for Learning" program, marketed with the help of the local PTAs. Five percent of subscribers' monthly payments is donated to local schools, with some of the proceeds used to setup homework hotlines and voice-mail boxes. (The inter-exchange carrier saved money on marketing as well.) A similar program has been launched by the Computer Learning Foundation (CLF) in conjunction with a major long distance carrier in eight pilot states. The Computer Learning Foundation is a nonprofit organization whose goal is to promote the effective use of technology to meet the needs of students, educators, and parents. The "Technology for Education Program—A Community Partnership," allows long distance customers to direct TechCredits to designated schools. TechCredits are earned by using long distance service. Schools may redeem TechCredits for computers, software, and other technology products available through a program catalog and selected by an independent panel of educators. Community-business partnerships such as these have the added benefit of promoting greater understanding and public support for education.

- Incentives for schools to be exporters of courseware to other educational organizations, and to video-on-demand commercial servers accessible to the broader educational community on a fee basis.

- Creation of research and development departments within schools or districts that develop materials with broader commercial applications and marketing departments to help sell them. This might add extra incentive to schools where future eligibility for additional grant opportunities is based on the original idea becoming self-sustaining.

Network Maintenance

Network connection and LAN maintenance could be financed through the vouchers and depreciation tax credits listed above. Deciding which subsidies could be designed and designated could be difficult. More likely, schools will have to pay for maintenance from their operating budgets. In view of the importance of budgeting for maintenance, however, schools might be required to present revised budgets that account for the costs of maintenance and support at the same time they receive funds for school and classroom connections. Furthermore, the cost of maintenance services might be reduced through purchasing cooperatives as suggested below.

U.S. TECH CORPS. The U.S. Tech Corps initiative, organized by the White House Office of Science and Technology Policy and officially launched in October 1995, presents one potentially successful model for supporting maintenance and training through public-private partnerships. Its stated mission is "to recruit, place, and support volunteers from the technology community who advise and assist schools in the introduction and integration of new technologies into the educational system." Volunteers from businesses with technological expertise provide assistance with local planning, technical support and advice, staff training, mentoring, and classroom interactions. The type of support would depend on the specific needs of a particular community. Activities might include getting local contractors to upgrade the wiring in a school, finding a volunteer systems administrator, or helping to develop a school's home page on the World Wide Web. The Tech Corps program is set to expand to all 50 states by the end of 1996.

Data Transmission

Once a school or classroom is connected to the outside switched telecommunications system, it remains problematic for the school to pay for the cost of voice and data transmission and for information services. Through the work of FOCAS member Senator Robert Kerrey and others, the needs of schools and libraries were addressed in the Telecommunications Act of 1996.

PREFERENTIAL RATES. The Snowe-Rockefeller-Exon-Kerrey amendment to the Act expands the universal service fund to include schools as beneficiaries for the first time. Under the Act, schools would gain access to telecommunications services at "incremental cost," saving schools from paying business or residential rates for telecommunications services. The universal service fund, redefined under the Act to include an ever-advancing level of technology beyond basic telephone service, will provide the subsidies enabling such discounts. Now, the Federal-State Joint Board on Universal Service convened under the Act is engaged in an examination of the types of services that should fall under the umbrella of universal service, and is searching for equitable formulas for determining preferential rates. Both traditional phone companies and newer service providers, such as cable companies, would pay into the universal service fund.

While it would be better to fund preferential rates out of general revenue, this approach does not appear to be politically feasible at the present time. However, with 93 percent of all Americans having basic telephone service, the universal service funding mechanism comes close to approximating funding out of general revenue and thus to placing the burden of educational network funding on those who benefit, all of society.

Cable companies have provided free basic cable service, commercial-free educational programming, and other curriculum materials through Cable in the Classroom for a number of years. Recently, AT&T has taken a step toward ensuring affordable rates for education by allowing schools free dial-up Internet service, browser software, and 100 hours of free usage as part of a $150 million commitment over the next five years. Other telecommunications companies are moving to offer free or lower cost Internet access to schools in the wake of AT&T's announcement.

There are a variety of online services that are directed at classroom use. The FOCAS task forces have not examined the prospects for reduced or free rates for commercial online services, but are mindful of several bulletin board type services aimed at the classroom for little or no cost. Many of these are supported by foundations (e.g., The JASON Project, funded by the JASON Foundation for Education), federal agencies such as the National Science Foundation or NASA, and other nonprofit or grassroots organizations (e.g., KIDLINK).

Teacher Training

Lack of teacher training is clearly one of the most significant barriers to the successful implementation of technology in the classroom and it is often omitted from funding proposals. Budgeting training as a line item in any technology purchase would appear to be a necessity. For example, according to FOCAS member Governor Gaston Caperton, the State of West Virginia appropriates approximately 30 percent of its budget for classroom technology to teacher training.

Furthermore, schools could develop matching programs that apply to training and software, not just direct funding. Equipment expenditures funded from external sources could be matched by content and teacher training funding by the schools, or vice versa, if it were easier for the schools to fund one or the other. This approach may make it more feasible for the schools to generate their matching funds. Similarly, if the school provides two teacher volunteers to train other teachers after school, then local businesses might also provide two people to do such training (see Tech Corps above).

Still other efforts could help in this regard, such as:

- Crediting a tax deduction for teachers who spend their own money on technology training.

- State tax credits to professional educators who meet state certification guidelines for proficiency in the use of technology.

- Private investment to establish training centers, such as the J. C. Sparkman Center for Educational Technology outside of Denver, Colorado, that cable operator TCI has established at its own cost. Other telecommunications companies have created similar training centers.

Creating a Responsive Local Technology Demand and Delivery System

Often, creating incentives for the fair and effective diffusion of technology in the schools involves the enhancement of the market system. Examples might include aggregating demand in order to effect bulk purchase of equipment, innovative and entrepreneurial activities by those not normally associated with such actions, and the intelligent use of research and development. Combining many of the suggestions of FOCAS task force participants, the following proposes three comprehensive components to enhance the local demand and delivery funding system:

- *Technology Purchasing Cooperatives* would be responsible for purchasing hardware, software, and support on a regional basis. These cooperatives could also coordinate and nurture funding relationships between school districts and local vendors for local technology centers.

- *Local Educational Technology Centers* would be primary conduit for grassroots demand aggregation and technology education, as well as a venue for vendor-school and lab-school interaction.

- *Technology Development Laboratories* could be assigned to reinvent curricula and school structure with respect to technological capabilities.

Technology Purchasing Cooperatives

Technology acquisition can benefit from the economics of scale. Purchases made on a regional rather than a state basis have, in general, realized price discounts of 3 percent to 5 percent. Regional purchasing groups have also contracted for comprehensive support services beyond what local districts can provide, an important factor in technology acquisition considering that support can cost more than five times what equipment costs. Regional cooperative price discounts are comparable to those currently available to large state buying consortiums, such as California's. But once initial inefficiencies and regulatory hurdles are worked out, regional cooperatives could offer both superior price and support.

Establishing a regional cooperative requires between two and twenty staff members, depending upon the personnel's familiarity with participating state funding and governing agencies. One example is the Southern Regional Education Board, covering the southeastern United States. Three other similar boards cover the west, midwest and northeast. These boards have long-standing reputations as credible, unbiased educational advocates. All four boards have long-standing, close relationships with state governments and agencies, making cooperative formation a logical extension. Originally focusing on cooperatives for higher education, most boards have begun branching out to include K–12 education purchases as well, providing opportunities for schools to utilize higher education's technology support resources.

Through communication and feedback with teachers at local centers, technology cooperatives could also serve as central collection, assessment, and rebuilding locations for recycled or donated equipment. The rebuilding function could also be used as a vocational activity for students at regional schools. Selective tax credits could provide an incentive for technology manufacturers and dealers to donate equipment the cooperative deems useful and government surplus technology could also be donated to the cooperatives.

To address the equity issue, families qualifying for Title 1 funds might be allowed to purchase recycled computers and modems from purchasing cooperatives for home use on low-interest installment purchase plans. With Title 1 subsidies, this could be an interest-free purchase plan.

Local Educational Technology Centers

Integral to the success of the purchasing cooperatives are mechanisms for local feed back, technical support, and teacher training. Local centers could be established in major population centers with the following four primary responsibilities.

(1) Develop technology purchasing packages, specifically software and hardware combinations. These packages could be shared with other local centers around the country for developing a set of annual "school standard" technology purchase packages, which would then be referred to the cooperatives for competitive bidding. Input could come from teachers and other educators during training sessions and special conferences, as well as from a small staff of professionals. In addition, technology centers and educational development labs could investigate cooperative educational technology projects with the Defense Advanced Research Projects Agency (DARPA) and other experienced educational technology users. Federal grants could be used for seed money for private vendor investment seeking to aggregate demand for their educational products.

(2) Providing just-in-time and in-service technology training for in-region teachers and administrators to familiarize them with the curricular uses of technology. This could be run by the regional educational laboratory if one were established (see below). As a first step, local administrators and teachers could create district and school-wide technology implementation plans.

Individual districts could be funded through dedicated budget percentages allocated for training. In some cases private investment might be found for the whole project, such as the J. C. Sparkman Center for Educational Technology mentioned earlier, or the Regional Technology Training Center in Baltimore, made possible by the Abell Foundation in cooperation with the State of Maryland.

(3) Provide technical/technology support for area schools, perhaps as a part of a purchasing cooperative contract. Funding would come indirectly from districts and other funding sources through purchasing cooperative contracts.

(4) Designate and operate a regional pilot school to demonstrate technology in action, to serve as a teaching model, and to examine curricular and technology reforms on a local level. Funding could come from state and federal grants and matching funds programs with private industry.

Technology Development Laboratories

Regional educational development labs could be responsible for developing curriculum and technology reforms. To do this, they would provide materials and design curricula for teacher and administrator training. The development labs could also work in conjunction with the nonprofit community and the Educational Testing Service (ETS) to develop new testing methods which reflect technology-assisted learning. Along with the local purchasing cooperatives, labs would use the local technology center as a locus for technology testing and local software development through teacher fellowships and development workshops.

Federal legislation enabling an expanded educational laboratory role already exists, albeit in a slightly different form. To effectuate this variation, it would be necessary to modify Title 3 of the Improving Schools Act in order to redefine educational consortia to accommodate local technology centers.

The combination of regional purchasing cooperatives, educational development labs and local technology centers creates a "support triangle" to support, maintain, and refine educational technology deployment while remaining sensitive to local control and regional variations.

TEACHER SUPPORT AND TRAINING

In a thorough review of the status of teachers' use of technology, the Congressional Office of Technology Assessment (OTA) observed, "To use new technologies well, teachers not only need access to them, but they also need opportunities to discover what the technologies can do, learn how to operate them, and experiment with ways to apply them."

Teachers, too, need to overcome some of the negative attitudes concerning technology that inhibit its incorporation into the classroom. Perhaps their caution can be forgiven to a certain extent. As Michael Timpane noted, "Teachers have been through the audio-visual revolution, then the television-as-savior revolution, so teachers are very skeptical. It is only lately that the technology was worth the effort." But it is clear that technology is not a replacement for the teacher. In fact, as Ervin Duggan commented, "No machine, no tool, no technology can succeed except in the hands of a talented teacher."

Training and Professional Development

Currently, schools spend 55 percent of their computer budgets on hardware expenses, 30 percent on software, and just 15 percent on training teachers how to use the technology. The technology training that does occur usually concentrates on the mechanics of using equipment, not on the more difficult aspects of how to work the technology into the curriculum. Furthermore, OTA reports that only six percent of elementary schools and three percent of secondary schools have a full-time computer coordinator to provide the necessary technical support to teachers using technology.

Generally speaking, teachers themselves are not great models of lifelong learners, and the reasons for this may be more structural than personal. It was agreed that the notion of professional development is not part of the teaching tradition in the United States, and that administrators and the public frequently reinforce the status quo. The primary barriers to professional development for teachers are time, place, money, and academic discipline. As one FOCAS member noted, teachers feel they need communion with disciplines.

It is difficult for teachers to keep up with the rapid pace of technological change. Teachers often lack the time to experiment with new technologies, attend training classes, and collaborate with other teachers to share ideas. They also frequently lack the support of school administrators who are concerned with standardized and easily quantifiable measures of student achievement. Learning that takes place through the use of technology may not be adequately reflected in the standardized tests and other traditional measures of academic progress. Furthermore, teachers are held accountable by administrators, parents, and their peers for improvements that may not be immediately apparent.

Needs

Teachers need help. In the face of these barriers, OTA reports that a substantial number of teachers report little or no use of computers for instruction. Although the situation is improving, most teachers have not had adequate training in using technology, especially in how to integrate technology into the curriculum and how to use technology to transform the learning and teaching processes. A first step toward improving the support given to teachers would be for schools and districts to allocate substantially more of the computer budget to training and support than is currently the case. Experienced technology-using school districts have recognized the need to make this very important investment in the human factor in technology. Some states, such as Florida, Texas, and West Virginia, are leading the way by requiring at least 30 percent of the computer budget to go to training teachers, and are also increasing the percentage of funds available for software and support.

While there are some new training programs that provide teachers with a thorough introduction to technology, many of these programs still do not go beyond the traditional models of teaching and learning. Teachers are uncomfortable giving up their traditionally authoritative role and allowing students to work more independently. With some exceptions, the materials now being produced for teachers generally do not go against that traditional model. Furthermore, the trend away from central office-based training to site-based educational administration and training makes it difficult to reach all teachers and leverage resources to design and implement successful training programs.

The "train the trainer" model, in which a cadre of teachers are trained in the use of technology and then sent back to their schools to train other teachers, has worked well in many areas, but it has its limitations. Because of a lack of technological support at most schools, the expert teachers are frequently pulled away from the classroom to act as troubleshooters when the technology breaks down. Expert teachers often resent being pulled away from their teaching to deal with technical problems.

To achieve sustained use of technology, and to use it well, OTA found that teachers need the following:

- *Visions* of the technologies' potentials;
- *Opportunities* to apply those visions;
- *Training* and just-in-time *support*; and

- *Time* to experiment and develop technology applications that fit their needs.[7]

Incentives

Creating incentives for teachers and administrators to learn about the new technologies and to incorporate them into the learning process is necessary to achieve "buy-in" from teachers. In presenting materials about the uses of new technologies in the learning process, teachers need to be able to see the advantages of teaching with technology without being threatened by the technology.

Visions, opportunities, training, support, and time are all powerful incentives that are capable of overcoming the barriers to the routine use of technology in the classroom. Additional incentives might motivate teachers to discover ways that technology can aid them as well. These include the following financial and professional incentives:

Financial Incentives

- increased compensation
- free or reduced cost access to technologies, especially the Internet
- personal tax credits for taking training courses

Professional Incentives

- giving each teacher a personal computer
- issuing "technology passports" or licenses that certify accomplishment in using technology in the classroom and serve as an additional certification of professional development
- embedding technology use in educational standards
- creating private sector internships for teachers
- offering peer recognition
- creating publishable materials
- improving the coordination of people and resources for training

- offering easier introductions to new models of technology

- creating a clearinghouse for technology information

- fostering greater public support for teachers who use technology

Collaborations

Businesses, governments, and the nonprofit sector can help create the incentives and resources to foster teachers' understanding and effective uses of these tools for learning. Through partnerships and collaborations, these sectors can help teachers overcome the barriers that stand in their way to successful integration of technology into student learning experiences. In particular, public-private resources should address the shortcomings of the current training models which include the lack of understandable and relevant information on learning technologies. In particular, businesses can help to provide the hands-on learning experience teachers need. Partnerships can also aid in the provision of time for teachers to experiment, and access to equipment and support personnel who can help teachers understand how to use technology effectively in their teaching practice and curriculum.

FOCAS members and their organizations are already involved in a variety of individual initiatives aimed at supporting teachers' and students' effective use of technology. Still, additional materials need to be developed for teachers to provide a broader array of informational resources. These should include human resources, media resources such as videotape, television or cable programming, CD-ROMs, and on-line services available through the Internet and the World Wide Web.

Teacher Technology Forum

Teacher technology forums can provide an opportunity for an exchange of information between educators and the communications and information industries. By bringing together in one location a cross-section of technology companies, video and multimedia providers, online services, teachers and educational administrators from the local, state and national levels, community service organizations, university professors, teachers unions, parent organizations, students, and other organizations that have expertise in this area, teachers might understand better what the technologies are, how they can be used, and offer new models for enhancing individual teaching and learning. Such forums would also enable industry to learn more about the specific needs and concerns of teachers, which could lead to collaborations and the development of new services to respond to the growing education market.

It is important that technology forums be local, focusing on the specific needs of a particular community. Teachers often face different obstacles from one community to another, which may require different approaches or applications for technology. They should include hands-on opportunities for experimentation, as well as discussions and sufficient resource people from the sponsoring organizations. Sessions could be structured in a variety of ways, including by technology or application, by skill level, or by subject matter.

Such forums should help educators (teachers and administrators) in developing a technology plan for their schools and thinking through the goals for technology in their particular localities. The sessions should engage teachers in this process. They should also push teachers and educators to think beyond the traditional methods and models of teaching, and into new models for teaching and learning. Forums should help to eliminate the fears and overcome the attitudinal barriers that hold many teachers back from adopting new technology in the classroom.

Internships, Fellowships, and Consultancies

Businesses and other organizations should establish programs to bring teachers and educational administrators into communications and information industry businesses as interns, fellows, and consultants. The teachers would have the opportunity for hands-on experience with technology, explore new uses for technology in the classroom, and gain a greater understanding of the social, economic, and technical changes brought about by the convergence of technologies. They could then share this expertise with their colleagues when they return to their schools. In return, businesses can gain direct, first-hand knowledge of the needs and interests of schools and teachers, an expanding market for technology and software. Duggan mentioned that PBS employs virtual interns to help develop the PBS Website.

INTERNSHIPS. A model internship program would involve teachers and administrators selected from local school districts for unpaid internships at communications and information businesses or technology-focused organizations during the summer months. These would be teachers and administrators with limited familiarity and knowledge of technology. They would work with middle or upper level staff in all areas of the organization, perhaps spending the entire time in one department for a more in-depth learning experience, or surveying several departments over the internship period. An optimal length for the internships would be two to four weeks.

FELLOWSHIPS. A fellowship program would select teachers with more familiarity and experience with technology in the classroom for paid fellowships at technology-oriented organizations during the summer months. If desired, the fellowships could be extended up to one year. The fellows would work with senior level staff in a single department or area of operation and would be given substantive work responsibility.

CONSULTANCIES. Businesses and other organizations with an interest in producing materials or equipment for the educational market are strongly encouraged to employ teachers and administrators from local school districts as consultants on individual projects.

Media/Multimedia Resources

There is a strong need for educators and technology companies to collaborate to create informational and instructional videotapes and CD-ROM materials for teachers. Information gathered at teacher technology forums could serve as a resource for the kind of information teachers need to have about technology. Additional videotapes could be produced as changes in technology warrant continual updating of skills and information, and as companies gain greater expertise in the ways that technologies can be used in learning.

Web Sites and Online Services

Another suggestion is a home page on the World Wide Web for teachers with questions about educational technology, including how to get started using technology, new ideas and applications, and a guide to resources within the community or across the nation. Many education-related Web sites offer descriptive information about the sponsoring organization's educational programs and products, but do not present more detailed information about how teachers can get started and integrate these resources into classroom use. A well-designed Web site could bring this information to teachers who are just starting to explore the Internet, and receive feedback from educators on their needs and problems.

Clearinghouse for Information on Educational Technology

There is a clear need for a clearinghouse for information on educational technology for teachers and administrators. Section 708 of the Telecommunications Act of 1996 creates such a clearinghouse in authorizing the National Education Technology Funding Corporation. Among its missions, the Corporation would "serve as a clearinghouse for information on new technologies." The Corporation would do this, in part, by promoting public-private partnerships. The Act, however, does not provide funding for the Corporation, although it permits the Corporation to receive both public and private donations. Alternatively, this could be a virtual clearinghouse, such as the Web site proposed above.

PROMOTING PUBLIC SUPPORT

All members of the community can play a vital role in promoting public support for education's effective use of communications and information technologies and services, increasing public awareness, and discussing local educational issues. Through public information campaigns with messages targeted at businesses, parents, and community leaders, and the expansion of Teacher Technology Forums to include members of the entire community, schools and their partners in the community can help to nurture a positive environment for technology in education.

Potential benefits include more informed educational policy and decision making at the local and state levels, support for building community-based technology platforms, and greater public understanding of the role of technology in supporting effective teaching and learning.

Increasingly, the public supports the integration of technology into the classroom. Still, there are barriers in public perceptions to be overcome. The following initiatives are suggested as a means to broadly disseminate information about the potential of technology for improving education.

Public Information Campaign

A coordinated campaign emphasizing the importance of technology to learning throughout a lifetime has the potential to make the greatest impact on informing and motivating people to support technology for America's school children. Any public information campaign must take into consideration the current environment and climate surrounding public discussions of education and technology today. This includes the current technological environment of schools, as well as the barriers to the effective use of technology in schools. In particular, it includes the public's strong concern for test scores and other traditional measures of student achievement.

A strategy for promoting public support through a public information campaign includes identifying the key stakeholders who need to be reached, crafting the messages that each audience needs to hear, and devising strategies and materials for disseminating those messages most effectively.

It is important to reach the appropriate stakeholders with well-designed information about the benefits of technology. These include businesses, parents, teachers, school administrators, community leaders, policymakers at all levels of government, foundations, the media, and higher education. Furthermore, emphasis should be placed on the responsibility of individuals to take advantage of learning and training opportunities, and the responsibility of corporations and organizations to support learning opportunities within their communities. Emphasis should also be placed on the responsibility of governments to ensure that opportunities for lifelong learning are available on an equitable basis.

Any public information campaign should also communicate the incentives for learning and the ways that technology can aid in the acquisition of new skills and knowledge. In every case, the message is that technology in schools, if used properly, can be a win-win situation for everybody concerned.

- Students benefit from increased self-motivation, discovery through simulation and exploration, and connection to new people and ideas.

- Society benefits because technology can provide equitable educational opportunities for all students, help people to develop lifelong learning skills, and make education relevant to daily life. The more students learn about the world, and the earlier they learn it, the better prepared they will be to participate in society.

- Teachers and administrators benefit because technology motivates students, makes more information and materials available in the classroom, creates home-school connections through e-mail, and increases administrative productivity.

- Businesses benefit from increased sales to schools and to the home, and from students who are prepared for the technology-rich workplace of the future. Well-trained workers make businesses more competitive, especially internationally. Businesses also receive the benefits associated with corporate goodwill in the community.

The following vehicles could be used to disseminate information about technology to the public.

Community Forums

Teacher Technology Forums can be expanded to involve members of the entire community to facilitate communication and understanding and promote partnerships. These forums would train and organize community information specialists and service providers to activate community grassroots efforts to support technology in the schools through community-based public-private partnerships. Such forums should involve members of local media as well, since they can serve an important public information function on education issues.

Public Service Announcements

Industry-subsidized public service messages should be developed for mass media, including local broadcasters, cable outlets, video news releases, movie theaters, and newspapers. These messages could be used to educate the public about the technology needs of schools. The Ad Council, which is launching a major, ten-year effort on the needs of children, could be an important participant in a PSA campaign. The public service campaign should increase awareness of the need to seek learning opportunities and to engage in lifelong learning in the changing economy. It should also articulate messages about the availability and relevancy of new tools and resources available for learning. It is particularly important to reach members of socially and economically disadvantaged groups who are in danger of being left behind without the skills necessary to function in the rapidly changing economy. Primetime placement is essential.

Opening School-based Technology Centers for Public Use After Hours

Parents and other members of the community who may not have computers or other technology resources in the home can benefit from technology in school-based technology centers. This would create an additional public resource for learning, one that is sadly underused as the equipment on which communities often spend a considerable amount of money sits idle after 3:00 p.m. If more people could benefit directly from technology in schools, it is likely that technology would enjoy greater public support rather than engender fear. There are, however, funding and policy obstacles to opening up schools after hours that must be dealt with. The centers could be staffed by members of the community or representatives from local technology-related businesses on a voluntary basis. School administrators may need some persuading when it comes to opening up the schools to the general public after hours.

Public Information Materials for the World Wide Web

There are many resources available for information on learning technologies. To the extent that these can be brought together into an electronic clearinghouse of information, perhaps on a World Wide Web site, such resources could reach a wider audience. Such a site could contain a directory for parents or others who have questions about what the Internet, or other technologies, have to offer education. It could also include a "what's hot" directory of information on educational technology materials.

Summary

The costs of connecting the schools go far beyond the acquisition and installation of hardware. Without the appropriate training for educators to use the technology, software to make the technology meaningful for learners, and technical support to maintain the systems, technological hardware loses its potent educational value. School administrators must look beyond funding hardware only (which has been the focus until very recently) and place greater emphasis on training, support, and the development of useful and effective software and applications for education. Likewise, members of the community must support educators in adapting the tools of the information age to classroom learning environments.

PART THREE:
TECHNOLOGY AND LEARNING
OUTSIDE THE CLASSROOM

The Need for a New Learning Environment

Part One of this report discusses the changing paradigm for learning, in which successful learning is certified by an individual's ability to apply the appropriate tools and information to the solution of problems encountered throughout a lifetime. This understanding is informed by a greater appreciation of the many ways in which individuals learn and the diverse environments in which learning takes place. Coupled with this shifting paradigm, the structural changes occurring in society highlight the need for a new learning environment.

The rapid rate of change in society continually challenges individuals and institutions to reinvent themselves in order to remain full participants in the economy and in society. In the new economy, some jobs are becoming obsolete and workers are faced with the prospect of learning new skills or becoming obsolete themselves. Moreover, changes in employment patterns no longer guarantee lifetime employment with one organization or even a single career path. Even those who trade in knowledge and information feel the pressure as such commodities and services change quickly. Consequently, the need for adult learning and retraining has grown significantly.

With demands for new skills and knowledge confronting individuals on a daily basis, it is clear that old models of classroom-based training will not suffice. People need more flexible learning environments that accommodate individual circumstances and styles of learning, luxuries the traditional classroom setting usually does not afford. They need opportunities for continuous learning that go beyond simple skills training, the model most prevalent now. Communications and information technologies are essential tools for adapting to a changing world. Perhaps most importantly, society needs a better understanding of and appreciation for the value of continuous learning outside the classroom. It is necessary to unlearn old habits and notions of how learning should take place, and develop new habits of learning that extend throughout a lifetime. And, there is a need to rethink how new opportunities for learning can be extended to all citizens.

Given the realities of daily life, much of this learning will have to take place outside traditional classroom settings. This final section presents an overview of the issues surrounding learning outside the classroom, with particular attention to the ways in which communications and information technologies might be used to facilitate lifelong learning and the potential obstacles to be encountered along the way. Unlike the preceding section of this report, the following discussion does not attempt to offer solutions as much as it seeks to inform public discussion of the complexities involved in building a society that values lifelong learning. FOCAS members believe that in raising public aware-ness of these important issues, leaders in business, government, and the nonprofit sector may begin to work together to create environments and resources that support continuous learning op-portunities for all.

A new environment for promoting the value of lifelong learning will acknowledge the following points.

Society needs to adopt an approach to learning that does not presume education stops when one receives a high school diploma or an advanced degree. As David Britt observed, "The approach of lifelong learning is different from our traditional approach to education, which is that you pack it into *x* number of years. After that, you are deemed educated. The philosophical underpinning of lifelong learning is radically different."

Conversely, education does not begin at age six, when a child enters elementary school. A new approach would instill the value of continuous, *lifelong* learning at an early age, and would promote opportunities for learning that meet the diverse needs of adults at all stages of their lives. "There is this conceit that the idea of lifelong learning starts at about age 21," Britt explained, alluding to the connection between childhood education and lifelong learning previously addressed in this report. "In fact, if you are really going to change the philosophy, you really have to introduce the concept of lifelong learning probably in preschool." Society must develop a different approach to preparing children for an economy that requires new and continuously changing sets of skills, *before* they enter the economy as full participants.

It is important to understand how people learn best, and adapt learning environments to meet these needs. Research on learning and cognitive processes has shown that context is integral to the learning process. Learning can occur in many different settings, both inside and outside the classroom. Effective learning experiences share three things in common: (1) effective learning is an active, goal-oriented process in which the learner is involved and engaged; (2) collaboration is important in learning, as much research has shown that learning is primarily a social process best accomplished through interaction with others; and (3) effective learning is a situated activity. That is, individuals learn best when they can understand and have a purpose.

Individuals must be motivated to learn and perceive lifelong learning as relevant to their lives. In other words, individuals need to be able to answer the question, *What's in it for me?* Alexander Kroll, CEO Emeritus of the advertising firm Young & Rubicam, offered some possible answers:

> Number one, to stay employed. Number two, to attain a better understanding or grasp of the world around me, and a deeper understanding of the events of my life. Number three, the ability to control my life and to control my destiny. I think control is a powerful and worrisome issue for most people. Fourth is a sheer sense of enjoyment. The ability to enjoy a broader range of what our culture has to offer. And last, the ability to play a role in constructing a more orderly and civil society.

FOCAS members determined that jobs, especially good jobs, are the principal motivation for people to learn. But the good jobs of the future will require a level and degree of sophisticated knowledge and standards higher than what is required today. "Can you imagine what a classified ad for an assembly line worker in the year 2000 will say?" Kroll asked. "It's not enough to know how to run a computer, you'll need physics as well. Getting a job is a technological issue and a lifelong learning issue. This is where the two issues come together."

Of course, education can provide additional benefits to the individual beyond the assurance of a decent job. Lifelong learning will mean different things to people at different stages of their lives. For some, lifelong learning is a way of addressing the spiritual component of one's life, the longing for personal growth, civility, and citizenship that exists regardless of economic condition. For others, it represents an inborn desire for competence and mastery. But most importantly, perhaps, learning must be seen as *relevant* to their lives.

The Barriers to Lifelong Learning

Promoting the value of lifelong learning will require efforts to overcome the structural, technological, and psychological barriers that stand in the way of individuals seeking to learn new skills and knowledge. Technology, if applied equitably, can be a powerful tool for overcoming these barriers.

As Michael Timpane noted, compared to other countries the United States has an enviable system of lifelong learning. "The way we conduct our formal education systems, you can have an *nth* chance, and many people take advantage of it. The average student age is 32 or 33 years old, with a large range around that. We're already quite a bit closer to lifelong learning than other nations." Indeed, the government secures a considerable amount of funds for student loans, and many corporations offer training for their employees and provide tuition reimbursement as part of employee benefits packages.

Yet not every person who wants to learn is served by this formal system at the time and in the manner which would be most beneficial. Fiscal constraints are forcing governments and businesses to cut back on money available for education. Furthermore, learning opportunities on the job frequently go to higher level workers who are already well educated, and do not reach many of the people who would benefit most. Statistics show that individuals with higher incomes and educational levels have greater access to continuous learning opportunities than others, and minorities receive less employer support on the job for education than their white counterparts.

In addition to limitations on their time, financial resources, and eligibility, geographic distance presents problems for other would-be learners. Adults with full-time jobs and families to support can find few extra hours during the week to focus on such activity, and even fewer dollars that are not already intended for their children's educations. Barriers of time, money, eligibility, and geography make it virtually impossible for some people to enroll in traditional institutions. Furthermore, the belief that learning must occur inside a formal educational structure is not often countered by the educational institutions that have traditionally defined the paradigm for learning. The idea that existing educational institutions (schools, colleges, and universities) alone can meet the learning needs of the changing economy is a dangerous fallacy.

In addition, many of the people in our society who have the greatest need for educational services are unable to articulate their need or to pay for services, whether as a result of disabilities, language barriers, or the simple fact that they have "dropped out" of society. There is an attitude that certain individuals cannot participate in the new economy, that some (e.g., the underclass) simply cannot make it in this world. Older members of the workforce, feeling unable to acquire new skills for the new economy, often pronounce themselves obsolete by subscribing to the adage "you can't teach and old dog new tricks." These and other factors create an uncertain market, making it difficult for capable organizations to create services.

There is also a lack of coordination among potential providers of learning services and resources in communities. Within organizations, there is sometimes a lack of leadership commitment to champion change to build and support new methods of learning. After all, training has often been a labor-intensive and expensive process, and the return on investments in training can be difficult to measure in the short term. The attitude exists among some corporations and organizations that education, training, and offering lifelong learning opportunities are not part the organization's responsibility.

Perhaps the most significant barriers to lifelong learning are the lack of coordinated public support and the prevailing public attitude about the relevance of education and learning to daily life.

As several FOCAS participants pointed out, this attitude is marked by a strong sense of economic pessimism regarding jobs and the economy, particularly in the wake of large-scale corporate layoffs and pervasive wage stagnation.

Public Attitudes Toward Education and Learning

For some people, learning is itself an enjoyable experience, and the joy of learning is sufficient motivation to seek new training or educational opportunities. For the majority of people, however, learning is frequently seen as a necessary but difficult task, often with limited relevance to the immediate concerns of daily life. This view is shaped by individual experience with the formal educational system and the public's perception that the system is not adapting to a changing world. "General support for public education is marginal," said Lloyd Morrisett, President of the John and Mary R. Markle Foundation. "Overall, Americans don't value high academic performance." Morrisett cited studies that show, by and large, adults volunteer for learning only when it relates to their job.

Alexander Kroll further described the public mood. "There's a great concern about the quality of schools at present," he noted. "We sense the values we want are not being delivered. [At the same time,] there's also an anti-intellectual strain in the national mood and an economic pessimism, both personal and in business."

A recent survey by the Public Agenda Foundation found that Americans do not place a high value on knowledge for its own sake. The survey describes the prevailing attitude in the United States as one that sees no payoff in learning advanced academic subjects, considers it unnecessary to teach great literature, and believes that socialization and athletics are a more important part of college. For many, too much learning is considered an elitist activity that sets one apart from the rest of the community.

In reality, however, lifelong learning is not elitist, and FOCAS members cautioned against adopting the notion that *all* learning must somehow suit utilitarian ends and answer practical questions of daily life. Ervin Duggan offered this "Athenian" vision of lifelong learning:

We really are talking about a vision of the good life here, and not just about jobs and economic competitiveness and the utilitarian's reasons for knowing things. That has to do with skills and information. But there is a whole spiritual dimension of our lives, there's the whole question of civility in our interactions with one another. There's the question of a vision of citizenship. And lifelong learning is key to all of those things if we are going to create a decent civilization, as well as decent economic lives for ourselves. It is not elitist to talk about it. We aspire to that civilized, good life for every human being regardless of their economic condition.

While this Athenian vision of lifelong learning may not be elitist, at times it may be viewed as a luxury. There is an underlying tension between learning in pursuit of "the good life" and the harsh realities encountered in people's daily lives. Most participants agreed that their own rationales for learning incorporated many aspects of the good life, yet conceded that such reasons might not hold for others. Morrisett articulated this tension:

Lifelong learning is something that people will engage in because it is challenging and enjoyable and a productive use of their time and spirit. At that extreme . . . for most people it's a luxury. It's a luxury in the sense that if you've got a good job, and if you've got leisure time, and if you've got enough money and nice surroundings, you can do that. On the other hand, the person who's worried about his job, or doesn't have enough resources, is trying to make ends meet, has all his time filled up, that sense of lifelong learning doesn't mean very much to him.

As he thought of trying to sell the Athenian concept of learning in the predominately rural communities his company serves, Jim Barr, President and CEO of TDS Telecommunications, observed, "Those are values that not everybody shares, however. I think everybody wants a good job, but we could be talking about people in western Tennessee whose greatest joy in life is shooting a raccoon. And they really are not caring about that Athenian approach."

In order to counter negative public attitudes toward learning, educators, businesses, and government must make the case for lifelong learning. Understanding the motivations and goals that individuals have is the first step on the path to expanding opportunities for lifelong learning and infusing technology as an important tool for those ends.

The Role of Technology

Communications and information technologies can play a vital role in meeting the diverse needs of individual learners. Technology can provide access to learning opportunities at any time, in any place, and in a variety of formats. Technology-based materials, which can be modularized and self-paced to respond to individual learning needs, offer unlimited opportunities for collaborative learning among groups and individuals working together to solve problems and reach common goals. It is important that both high-tech and low-tech options be available, in recognition of the fact that learners do not all share equal technical competencies, nor do all learning needs require a high degree of technological sophistication.

Technology can expand opportunities for learning and empower individual learners by:

- delivering more opportunities for learning to more people, more efficiently, at potentially lower cost;

- promoting the value of individual creation and distribution by permitting people to share their own learning process and results with others, motivating learners in the process;

- connecting people to each other and facilitating greater cooperation and collaboration among communities, individuals and institutions;

- overcoming some time and distance barriers;

- improving productivity; and

- bringing a personal connection to learning not possible before, through self-pacing, just-in-time learning, nonthreatening learning environments (through levels of anonymity), and the accommodation of various learning styles.

Communications and information technologies also create channels to enable people to participate more easily in public policy and political issues, debates, and action at the local, state, and national levels. Technology has the added benefit of assisting institutions (governments and businesses) in becoming more relevant, open, and productive, as well as more consumer, client, and employee driven.

With the aid of technology, learning can occur outside of classrooms, through different kinds of institutions, in the workplace, in the home—anywhere that communications and information technologies are present. Technology employed for learning outside the classroom can have all of the same benefits that apply in a classroom setting: it can aid in the development of new skills, job opportunities, and the pursuit of knowledge. But it can only do this if the appropriate technological resources are developed and they are accessible to all.

Developing Community-based Resources for Learning

Developing Technological Tools

Promoting the development of technological resources for individual and community-based learning, and ensuring access to these resources are important components of a strategy for promoting lifelong learning. Essentially, this means developing community-based information and navigation tools that can assist individual learners or organizations with technology-based learning. Particular attention should be given to creating access points to information resources in the places where people already gather. Additional emphasis should be given to overcoming technological obstacles, including the fact that many potential technological resources for learning are not user friendly and are not application-focused. The lack of interoperability and the fact that the National Information Infrastructure is not fully deployed present additional barriers.

Creating a Clearinghouse of Initiatives

FOCAS members suggest that a starting point to building communities of lifelong learning would be the establishment of a clearinghouse that is both national in its reach and local in its relevance to the emerging information needs of the public. Such a clearinghouse could be charged to identify, evaluate, and promote learning and technology initiatives that work in communities. The public library might be its site and prototype. Recruiting and training professionals to help provide a community information service should also be developed. Such a center could serve as a one-stop advisory service for people to learn about ways to use technology for learning, from low-technology (such as telephone-based services) to high-technology (such as computer and Internet services).

Developing an Information Inventory Index

Likewise, achievable indicators for individual and community access to information technology, training, and tools might be developed. These indicators would include reasonable expectations for the achievement of community-wide levels of information literacy. Indicators of this kind would allow evaluators and advocates to judge if appropriate progress is being made over time within individual communities, and avoid ending promising programs prematurely. From these indicators, communities could form an Information Inventory, similar to other indices that establish measures for performance, evaluation, and quality of life. For example, how many homes have personal computers? Does a community have cable access and local cable channels? Does the library offer public training or technology for Internet access? Do the community's media expand the citizen's awareness of an information economy? The goal is to try to make operative the concept of access to lifelong learning.

Building a Society that Values Lifelong Learning

There are at least three primary beneficiaries of a society that values continuous learning. First, there is the individual, who not only becomes a more marketable worker, but also benefits from the self-discovery and self-development that accompanies learning. Second, the economy and its constituent organizations benefit from a workforce that is more skilled, productive, and competitive. Finally, democratic society and its institutions reap rewards from the participation of better informed, more knowledgeable citizens.

It is important, therefore, to communicate the need for life-long learning in the new global information society, emphasizing the responsibility of individuals to take advantage of learning and retraining opportunities, the incentives they have for doing so, and the responsibility of corporations and organizations to offer and support opportunities for learning on the job and within their communities.

Equally important is the development of technological resources for individual and community-based learning, and insurance of access to these resources. Particular attention should be given to creating access points to information resources in the places where people already gather, such as the workplace, libraries, and community centers. Furthermore, it is essential to identify the resources within a community that individuals may turn to for help in using technology resources for learning.

Finally, none of this can happen without financial resources. New incentives for investments in human capital and training will have to be identified and new strategies for funding the development of and access to technological tools for learning will be required. However, any efforts in this regard must be guided by the following four principles. First, communities and individuals cannot rely solely on government funding. Second, communities and individuals cannot rely on business altruism either, but on what is good for businesses. Third, it is important to remember that individuals will use resources to which they have access and which are sensitive to their learning needs. Finally, all initiatives must be economically sustainable and scalable.

Everyone—individuals, businesses, governments, and non-profit organizations—has a role to play in realizing the vision of a society that values lifelong learning. Governments provide the focus. They can direct attention and distribute limited resources to the areas that need attention, opportunities, and resources. Businesses provide the levers. They can seed initiatives, identify critical needs, and provide employment opportunities and rewards for learning (e.g., jobs, promotions, etc.). Individuals pull the levers. They will identify and take advantage of the opportunities provided, sometimes creating those opportunities themselves, and help determine which resources are needed. The nonprofit sector, especially community-based organizations, can provide bridges to connect individuals to the opportunities that will enable them to become lifelong learners.

If technologies are to be put to the most beneficial uses, we need to design better uses, develop better policies, and understand the impact that they have on society. Most importantly, we need strong leadership from business, government, and the nonprofit sector, working in collaboration to lead us in the right direction.

ENDNOTES

1. "Advanced Telecommunications in U.S. Public Schools, K–12," U.S. Department of Education, February 1995.

2. The specific costs associated with each area are not easily determined. Among the studies that have attempted to quantify these costs is a U.S. Department of Education Working Paper, "Connecting K–12 Schools to the NII: A Preliminary Assessment of Technology Models and their Associated Costs" by Russell Rothstein.

3. Although remanded by the courts for further comment, the proposed social contract has the potential to bring technology into the learning environments of a significant number of children.

4. The McGuffey Project is a private sector initiative staffed by National Strategies, Inc., a consulting firm in Washington, DC. The project agenda includes the instigation and support of legislation to accelerate the networking of classrooms.

5. A state-based alternative to universal service funds is to use similar subsidy funds established by state Public Utility Commissions. Some states are considering this approach.

6. Figures are based on California excise tax revenue extrapolations. All figures in 1995 dollars.

7. U.S. Congress, Office of Technology Assessment, *Teachers and Technology: Making the Connection*, fact sheet.

Appendices

Appendix
Societal Goals
Working Group Report

This report is the product of the Societal Goals working group, which formed at the Tenth Annual Aspen Institute Conference on Telecommunications Policy in August of 1995 in Aspen, Colorado. The group continued its work through the fall of 1995, and developed the Education Telecommunications Council initiative outlined below. This report contains additional information on past and current telecommunications and cable industry initiatives to promote the effective use of technology in schools. This report appears in the Appendix of the forum report of the conference, The Communications Devolution: Federal, State, and Local Relations in Telecommunications Competition and Regulation *(The Aspen Institute, 1996).*

From August 6–10 of 1995, The Aspen Institute held its Tenth Annual Conference on Telecommunications Policy, convening a small group of leaders from the telecommunications policy community. Local exchange companies, cable companies, consumer representatives, academics, and federal, state, and local government decision-makers attended. The societal goals working group was charged with identifying the social goals that telecommunications policy and regulation should seek to achieve. The working group determined that ubiquity of access to the tools of telecommunications technology should be a primary societal goal and that the telecommunications industry should play a role in providing such access. Working group members also agreed that, given our increasingly information based society, it is imperative that the nation prevent the creation of a new class of technological have-nots. The working group concluded that an essential step towards meeting the goal of ubiquitous access is to equip public schools (K–12) and libraries with telecommunications technology and provide access to that technology.

In analyzing the goal of ubiquitous access, the working group recognizes that contributions from telecommunications providers are not the only contributions needed to achieve the goal. We do not believe that achievement of the goal should be the responsibility of one industry; rather, it is the responsibility of the entire nation. Indeed, we recognize that the demand side—the educational sector—must play the primary role in developing applications, obtaining and maintaining equipment, and training teachers in the use of the applications. These aspects, however crucial, are beyond the focus of the working group. In our view, the task of the telecommunications and related industries is to serve speedily and effectively the needs of the educational sector. To the extent that the telecommunications industry continues to make contributions towards the national goal, such contributions should be coordinated in a manner that maximizes their efficacy in preparing the nation and our children for the information age.

There is one further preliminary observation: We do not think it appropriate for this working group to comment on the pending (and, we note, still shifting) legislative proposals in this field.

After identifying our primary societal goal, the working group analyzed how telecommunications providers have responded thus far to the call to prepare our citizens to use advanced technology in accessing information. Each segment of the telecommunications industry represented in the working group described their individual contributions to education in the attached summary. While this is not an exhaustive survey of the industry, it does provide a fairly comprehensive overview of the role that the industry can play in achieving the goal. Briefly, the industries include:

- *Cable Companies.* Cable television has dedicated considerable resources to ensure that children are an integral part of the information revolution. The cable industry has provided human resources, programming, and equipment to schools so that teachers and students may experience first-hand the benefits of broadband communications networks. Cable companies are continuing to develop instructional programming and teacher support materials.

- *Interexchange Carriers (IXCs)*. For interexchange carriers, the areas of distance learning, videoconferencing, and Internet access have received particular emphasis. The IXCs offer a vast array of National Information Infrastructure-related products and services to the education community. These services range from a simple telephone in the classroom to technology as complex as a full-motion interactive distance learning network. In addition to offering products and services, IXCs have contributed products, services, and expertise.

- *Local Exchange Carriers (LECs)*. A United States Telephone Association (USTA) survey that covered about half of the local exchange industry found that recent and near term planned expenditures for providing community and school sites with access to the National Information Infrastructure (NII) totaled hundreds of millions of dollars and covered over 40,000 sites across the nation.

As we analyzed the contributions being made by telecommunications providers, it became clear that, although many are contributing, the contributions are occurring on an erratic basis, without coordination and perhaps not always in the most effective manner. While the telecommunications industry has contributed millions of dollars to help provide information access to public schools, the contributions have been somewhat ad hoc, at times redundant, and not always responsive to the needs of schools and libraries. Although educators understand the potential value of information technology in the learning process, and telecommunications providers understand the technology, the entities often may not truly understand each other. We conclude that there is a need for a forum in which the telecommunications industry, joined by interested educators and government representatives, can discuss the telecommunications needs of our citizens.

The working group proposes that such a forum should be convened under government auspices, thereby enabling government to serve as a catalyst to focus the efforts of industry to assist in serving the educational needs of the nation. The governmental auspices would also give assurance against any concerns on antitrust grounds. While it is reasonable to rely primarily upon open markets and free competition to produce the benefits of the information revolution, the working group concluded that government has a role as catalyst. Part of this function includes facilitating the exchange of information regarding possible options and contributing towards the implementation of a national information infrastructure. The group concluded that:

- A government coordinator could serve to bring together the major telecommunications industry players and other interested parties so that, to the extent possible, all options can be entertained and understood by those entities seeking to maximize the usefulness of advanced technology to access information.

- Because a fair and equitable distribution of the benefits of the information revolution is not a foregone conclusion, the attention of a government coordinator is most helpful to ensure a nationwide implementation of the information infrastructure.

- To the extent the government will act by necessity to encourage access to advanced technology, the input of industry and the education sector to that process should be more coordinated.

The Committee for Economic Development (CED) issued a similar call for increasing the coordination and involvement of business, education, and government in order to make information technology more accessible to children.* CED stated that business,

---

* The Committee for Economic Development is a nonprofit, nonpartisan independent research and policy organization of some 250 business leaders and educators. This recommendation was contained in its September 1995 report, "Connecting Students to a Changing World: A Technology Strategy for Improving Mathematics and Science Education."

government, and education should develop partnerships with public schools to share resources, knowledge, and technology. They further provided that the ability to access information should no longer be considered an educational frill; it should be recognized as a necessary part of education and, therefore, an essential item in the regular school budget. Their report recognizes that increased competition among providers will ultimately result in fairer pricing for all, but such competition will take time to take hold, and schools need more affordable access now. CED called on federal, state, and local policymakers, in cooperation with the private sector, to develop new incentives and strategies so that schools can gain affordable access to communications services. In addition, CED stated that any strategies that are developed to provide affordable access to schools should ensure that costs are shared.

We believe that the Federal Communications Commission (FCC) is the government entity best equipped to take on such a task. The Network Reliability Council, established by the FCC in 1991 to address national reliability concerns, should serve as a model for how the FCC could effectively work towards meeting the goal of maximizing the usefulness of telecommunications in preparing children for the information age. The Network Reliability Council successfully assembled diverse groups to study a particular problem, recommend solutions, and find effective ways to implement those recommendations.

If the FCC were to establish an Education Telecommunications Council to address the telecommunications needs of the nation's elementary and secondary schools and libraries, it would call on representatives from local exchange companies, interexchange companies, cable companies, cellular companies, computer firms, software developers, educators, and state and local governments. In this manner, the Education Telecommunications Council would be expected to partner with educational agencies and serve as an impartial central clearinghouse so that the efforts of the telecommunications industry in the educational field are subject to appropriate coordination and carried out in a way that most effectively meets the needs of the educational sector. Thus, entities that seek to maximize the usefulness of advanced technology to access information would be able to make more fully informed decisions.

The Education Telecommunications Council, as an impartial central coordinator, would thus be expected to contribute to the implementation of a truly nationwide information infrastructure.

INDUSTRY CONTRIBUTIONS

I. Cable's Contribution to Education

Cable television has dedicated considerable resources to ensure that students are an integral part of the information revolution. The cable industry has voluntarily provided people, programming, and equipment to schools so that teachers and students may experience firsthand the benefits of a broadband communications network.

Many cable television companies are developing instructional programming and teacher support materials, connecting schools, providing distance learning, and contributing audiovisual equipment, teaching guides, and satellite dishes at cost. Cable companies are buying copyright clearances on behalf of educators and training administrators, teachers, students, and parents to effectively incorporate new educational delivery technologies, equipment, programming, and software into the classroom environment.

Connecting Schools

Thirty-two national cable networks have teamed up with more than 7,200 local cable systems to create Cable in the Classroom, a public service initiative of the cable television industry. Through Cable in the Classroom, the cable industry has invested more that $320 million to provide more that 70,000 schools (70 percent of public and private schools) with the "Information Superhighway" at their doorsteps. Through cable connections provided free of charge, four out of five students—numbering some 38 million—receive direct access to many of the electronic services on the information superhighway and more than 525 hours per month of educational, commercial-free programming. Teachers also receive complimentary curriculum-related support materials and Cable in the Classroom magazine, a monthly publication that lists upcoming educational programs by subject area. A 1995 technology survey conducted for Cable in the Classroom and four other national education groups indicated 58 percent of the teachers surveyed regularly use the Cable in the Classroom resources in their classrooms.

Training

Research has shown that teachers are more likely to use resources like Cable in the Classroom if they have been trained in the application of such resources to the curriculum. The cable industry has sponsored thousands of hours of training for educators during teacher "in-service" sessions. Books, videotapes, and lesson plans are available to schools at no charge.

The J. C. Sparkman Center, developed by TeleCommunications, Inc. (TCI), is a state-of-the-art training facility in a special digital satellite transmission center where educators, school administrators, and parents get hands-on training with cable-delivered resources in a variety of technologies, including computer and CD-ROM applications, information access, multimedia development, desktop video conferencing, and video disc technology. Three hundred and seventy scholarships were financed by TCI in 1995. The average participant cost is $2,500, or 10 times the annual expenditure on teacher training nationwide.

Through The Family and Community Critical Viewing Project, a collaboration of the National Parent Teacher Association, National Cable Television Association, and Cable in the Classroom, cable operators are conducting hundreds of workshops helping parents and children become smarter television viewers. To assist parents in this effort, Continental Cablevision developed an award-winning bimonthly magazine, Better Viewing, which lists quality children's programming by age and provides tips on using television productively in the home.

Interactive and Distance Education

Satellite-based distance learning networks like Mind Extension University (ME/U) have been developed by cable companies to provide quality instructional education to remote locations. Media General Cable and the Fairfax, Virginia public school system have the only "local" distance learning program created by K–12 educators to serve teachers and students nationwide. As many as 13,000 schools have participated in this network drawing on the talents of exemplary teachers and innovative instructional designers to create more that 250 hours of instructional, enrichment, and staff development programming with unlimited taping and duplication rights.

Using their broadband capacity, local cable operators have expanded distance learning opportunities to include two-way audio and video, allowing students in remote locations to see and hear their teachers and originating teachers to see and hear all their students.

For example, Cox Cable Communications wired Clear View Elementary School in San Diego, California directly to its headend with fiber optics so fourth graders regularly access an electron microscope at San Diego State University, 26 miles away, as they study the scientific process in their science curriculum. While studying the 50th anniversary of V-E Day, second to sixth grade students joined fiber optically with Nebraska and Rhode Island students for a two hour video conference to share stories and information with students in Shevington, England. Teachers, student teachers, and master's degree students use the connection with San Diego State University for remote instruction.

TCI initiated a showcase school project in Carrollton City, Georgia where schools teach Spanish daily to all 1,700 elementary students with only two teachers. Each building has its own local area network; two dozen CD-ROM drives and 25 file servers provide interactive access in every classroom to all the instructional resources of the district and to administrative services. Stand alone multimedia workstations capture video network still images for student projects. Simultaneously, a separate cable video network links the district's classrooms.

After a year of planning and investing more that $135,000, Continental Cablevision created a fiber optic system for Lincoln High School, Brookside Elementary School, and the San Joaquin County School Administrative offices to allow multipoint data transmission between science classrooms, the Library, Administrative Building, and Performing Arts Building, as well as traditional downstream data transmission. In addition, a local area network and wide area network were created to enable Internet connections to every classroom as well as an interactive video network.

A partnership between Time Warner and United Telephone Service of Ohio links disadvantaged school districts with those that can provide needed resources. A two-way video and audio optical fiber network links three high schools and a vocational school and is used for distance learning courses in creative writing, employability skills, and Spanish language. It is also used for video conferences among teachers, principals, superintendents, and boards of education, as well as for adult education programs.

Cable operators in several states are working together to build statewide, interactive fiber optic networks. For example, the goal of "Fiber-Span Pennsylvania" is to link existing satellite, microwave, coaxial, and fiber resources through a statewide fiber network in order to provide quality education to all schools. The project will eventually interconnect all the cable systems in the state.

Many cable companies have constructed Institutional Networks (I-NETs) that are discreet interactive broadband networks separate from the home subscriber's cable network. I-NET usually serve specific schools, municipal offices (police and fire departments), and hospitals and are very effective in carrying point-to-point voice, data, and video signals. For example, in Continental Cablevision's New England region, more than 100 municipalities and 500 schools can use the I-NET free of charge for their video needs.

With free access to the I-NET provided by Continental Cablevision and TCI, six local high schools in the Chicago suburbs of Rolling Meadows, Buffalo Grove Village, and Elk Grove Village can hold face to face conversations with teachers and students 15 miles away. Purchasing similar multichannel transmission facilities from another source would easily exceed $10,000 a month.

Cable makes multidimensional contributions to education through the efforts of cable operators to build distance learning networks, the products of program networks like The Discovery Channel and ME/U, which are exclusively dedicated to education, and industry-wide initiatives like Cable in the Classroom. Utilizing existing INETs, fiber optics, coaxial cable, satellite, and computer technologies, cable enables teachers to transcend classroom walls and allows isolated and economically disadvantages students access to learning.

II. IXC's Contributions to Education

The interexchange carriers (IXCs), along with the regional Bell operating companies (RBOCs), cable companies, and others, are busy delivering the message that technology can improve the education process and reduce costs. For IXCs, the areas of distance learning, video conferencing, and the Internet receive particular emphasis.

The IXCs offer a vast array of NII-related products and services to the education community, for example, long distance and wireless service, telephone and advanced communications systems, audio and video teleconferencing, interactive community-based learning networks, and voice mail and advanced voice processing services. Ranging from a simple telephone in the classroom to something as complex as a full-motion interactive distance learning network, IXCs are bringing the power of technology and advanced communications solutions to the classroom.

IXC involvement in education is multifaceted and includes support for public policy initiatives, contributions of money, products, and services and expertise, and sponsorships and exhibits. In addition to supporting a long term, strategic commitment to education, these activities provide benefits to the IXC in the form of brand recognition as well as through recognition for helping the community, advancing education, and being technology leaders.

The activities range from donations of hardware and software to the sale of products and services specifically designed for schools. A summary review of the IXC activities is perhaps the best way to illustrate the scope and depth of the IXC commitment to education.

AT&T

AT&T supports ($150 million) education for business and philanthropic purposes. Realizing that no one organization can do it all, AT&T is focusing on four areas: teacher support, parental involvement, technology, and the fields of math, science, and engineering. In addition, AT&T recently announced it would provide three months of free Internet access to all schools in the United States.

A few illustrative examples of AT&T's involvement in education are listed below:

- The Telstar 4 family of satellites marked the beginning of a new era in "distance learning," including the virtual college as represented by the National Technological University (NTU) and the Satellite Educational Resources Consortium (SERC) for schools.

- In five major cities, the "Teachers for Tomorrow" program helps prepare new teachers for the unique challenges of inner-city schools.

- The "Teacher & Technology Institute" brings together outstanding math and science teachers from across the country to share in a two-week hands-on learning experience in using the latest technologies.

- A trial project in North Carolina links three rural schools via Integrated Services Digital Network (ISDN) technology to the interactive distance learning program at Appalachian State University.

- Substantial financial support is provided for a PBS program called Mathline, a satellite-based service which delivers instructional videos to schools.

- AT&T collaborated in the design of showcase Centers for Excellence in Education which offer the newest educational technologies for teachers to explore how innovative technology can improve the way teachers and students learn.

- Voice processing systems and homework hotlines are available to support parental involvement.

- The ImagiNation Network enables parents and students nationwide to work together on-line on homework assignments.

MCI

Examples of MCI's involvement in education include:

- Elementary school students in New Jersey take their first field trip to Australia using Internet technology.

- A demonstration distance learning project of the "classroom of the future" shows how school districts can share teachers, classrooms, and resources to improve education and cut costs.

- Grants are given to libraries to provide access to the Internet.

- MCI provides a new 155mb/s Very high-speed Backbone Network Service linking five supercomputer centers in the United States.

- MCI set up four "electronic classrooms" with full broadcast quality video conferencing equipment at an Arizona university;

- Middle school students get help with homework using a toll-free homework hotline staffed by teachers.

- Colorado University students are given an ID card with a picture on the front and a magnetic stripe on the back. In many ways this multipurpose card acts as a key to the university, i.e., access to campus facilities and events, paperless checking account, food services charge card, long distance calling card, etc.

Sprint

A few examples of Sprint's educational activities include the following:

- A competition is sponsored among high schools which challenges students to solve a problem using advanced data communications tools.

- Eighteen schools in Tennessee use a fiber optic network to provide full-motion, real-time interactive television for distance learning instruction and collaboration among students and teachers. This network is also used off-hours by businesses for worker skill training and for health education seminars.

- A voice response system allows teachers to quickly and easily record messages telling parents of the day's events or homework assignments. In turn, parents can dial in and leave messages, eliminating the writing of notes and playing phone tag.

- Selected educational videos are available to eight California elementary schools equipped with "video jukebox" access to the Information Superhighway.

- Wide area networks allow students to link up with research centers and libraries across the country.

III. LEC's Contributions to Education

Similar to both cable and IXCs, local exchange carriers have actively supported educational efforts. A USTA survey that covered about half the LEC industry found that recent and near term planned expenditures on providing community and school sites access to the NII totaled hundreds of millions of dollars and covered over 40,000 sites. The range of these education efforts are illustrated by just a few selected examples from the four companies listed below.

Ameritech

In Indiana, Ameritech is developing and connecting networks of video telecommunities capable of curriculum sharing, electronic field trips, collaborative learning, and school-to-business involvement. Ameritech has committed to invest up to $120 million over the six year period from 1994 to 2000 for broadband infrastructure support. This investment will provide digital switching and transport facilities including, where appropriate, fiber optic facilities, to every interested school, hospital, and major government center in the company's service area on a nondiscriminatory basis.

In addition to the infrastructure commitment, which could reach nearly 2,000 schools in Indiana, Ameritech is donating $30 million over that same period to a nonprofit organization, the Corporation for Educational Communications (CEC), for services and hardware for video distance learning. The CEC grants will provide classroom work-stations and large screen monitors to approximately 550 middle schools, high schools, and universities throughout the state. All public, private, and parochial schools serving grades 7 through 12, located in Ameritech-Indiana service areas, and accredited by the State Department of Education are eligible for grants. Not only will CEC provide the extensive video distance learning hardware, but it is financially supporting the schools through usage and wiring grants, and the hiring of educational planners and trainers. Also, significant resources are invested in the development of cultural and educational interactive content for the video network to support the stated needs of the education community. In its first year of operation, 40–50 different organizations have installed video distance learning service that can connect to almost 150 educational and cultural institutions within Indiana. Demand for service continues to grow quickly due to the CEC financial support and push for collaborative planning among different schools districts.

In Ohio, a similar commitment is underway. By the end of year 1999, Ameritech has committed to make available broadband services to all state chartered high schools, including vocational technical schools, colleges, and universities. This is over 550 locations. Additional commitments to libraries and government locations extend the capability to nearly 1,100 locations.

In Wisconsin, by the end of year 1998, Ameritech has committed to extend broadband facilities to the doorstep of every secondary and technical school, university, and college in the Ameritech service areas. With additional commitments to libraries and government centers, over 600 locations will be wired for broadband access.

An additional $11.5 million matching funds grant for Michigan will provide customer premises equipment, servers, workstations, and library automation support. In a program labeled Education Avenue, Ameritech has offered to extend dial-up or dedicated Internet access to the first 500 schools who choose to use this service. Ameritech will provide equipment and routers, connections to an Internet provider, and will heavily discount the use of the service in its first year and a half of operation. A grant to Michigan State University will develop curriculum lesson plans utilizing Internet resources.

Bell Atlantic

WORLD SCHOOL, AT WEST VIRGINIA PUBLIC SCHOOLS. Bell Atlantic of West Virginia is providing public schools with the staff development, software, mid-level provider fees, and some network equipment to connect at high speed a minimum of five personal computers (PCs) per school to the Internet. To participate in this voluntary program, schools are responsible for acquiring their own PCs, arranging teacher development time, inside wiring, and providing either token ring or ethernet terminal adapters. Bell Atlantic provides robust software for each PC and the school router that allows Internet traffic to piggyback the West Virginia Electronic Information System (WVEIS) 56kb/s frame relay network used by school administration for student demographics, performance records, and guidance. The $10 million project should be completed by the end of 1997. Of the 790 schools in the state, 650 already are using WVEIS. Bell Atlantic is providing training to teachers in about 25 schools each month. Already teachers have begun exciting curriculum projects over World School.

BASIC EDUCATION CONNECTION. In January 1994, Bell Atlantic made a commitment to connect every public elementary and secondary school to video dialtone and Internet when the neighborhood served by the school has access to the full service network. At Bell Atlantic shareowner expense, each school would be given access to educational programming available in the video dialtone environment. An estimated 10,400 public schools will benefit from this commitment.

BELL ATLANTIC AND UNION CITY COLLABORATE ON SUCCESSFUL MULTIMEDIA LEARNING FOR CHILDREN. The highly successful multimedia learning environment developed in children's homes and the Christopher Columbus School in Union City, New Jersey, is widening and the improvement in test scores associated with the multimedia environment is strengthening. The turnaround in academic performance shown in Christopher Columbus school began after a crisis five years ago. At that time, Union City test scores, absenteeism, dropout rates, and other measures of school performance were so dismal that the state was threatening to take over the school system. The school system, parents, and teachers vowed to rescue the schools from that fate. Their innovative five-year plan included exactly the kind of boost in learning, improvements in teacher performance and attitude, and participation by parents that the partnership with Bell Atlantic has made possible.

DELAWARE: DISTANCE LEARNING TAKES SHAPE. Bell Atlantic of Delaware (BA-DE) and the State of Delaware are harnessing the statewide fiber optic network currently under construction to make better learning opportunities available to K–12 students and teachers. For the current school year, two school districts used two-way video distance learning technology for courses such as algebra, Spanish, and philosophy and for staff development programs. Following this success trial, a tariff for distance learning has been filed and more schools have asked to be linked. BA-DE successfully bid on connecting all public schools to the Internet, which will be done quickly using Switched Multi-Megabit Digital Service (SMDS). Based on educational market enthusiasm and feedback, BA-DE is also working on the business case to create a market trial of networked multimedia applications. Networked multimedia was the technical cornerstone for the highly successful results in Union City, New Jersey. As in Union City, BA-DE works collaboratively with teachers, school boards, and other public officials toward the best learning opportunities. Children seem to benefit greatly from good technology and public-private collaboration.

BellSouth

Using BellSouth facilities, Palm Beach County, Florida deploys commercial quality broadcast signals that currently reach eight high schools, one community college, and two administrative centers for distance learning applications.

Charlotte's Web is a comprehensive infrastructure and network of services in the Charlotte-Gastonia, North Carolina and Rock Hill, South Carolina area to provide citizens and school children with free access to information and educational resources. Corporate partners include BellSouth, Time Warner Cable, and Vision Cable. Charlotte's Web provides informational, educational, and communications services including medical help and referral services, on-line library services, and distance learning.

In its efforts to bring modern communications technologies into the classroom, BellSouth Mobility has introduced ClassLink™, a mini-cellular system to provide students access to educational and cultural resources. The system also allows teachers to communicate with colleagues outside the classroom, improving the productivity of teachers and staff. The system is especially appropriate for rural schools or in facilities that cannot be retrofitted for modern technology.

NYNEX

NY NET/THE LIVING TEXTBOOK (a collaborative trial between Syracuse University and NYNEX). An ATM network links Syracuse University, Cornell University, Rome Labs, Columbia University, and several other higher education sites. Syracuse University and other schools are working together to better understand how multimedia technology can be integrated into the classroom curriculum. The Living Textbook is a trial of multimedia software over the Asynchronous Transfer mode (ATM) network in the K–12 segment; the project links the Ralph Bunche School in Harlem, Fowler High School in Syracuse, Rome Free Academy in Rome, and Whitesboro Middle School near Utica to the Internet, the computers of Syracuse University's Northeast Parallel Architectures Center (NPAC), and research facilities at the U.S. Air Force Rome Laboratory. The students at the various schools can see and talk to each other, while simultaneously working on the same project.

NYCLASSNET. NYClassNet is a digital two-way audio and video distance learning network that connects four New York City high schools, Manhattan Community College, and Lincoln Center to deliver college courses, share teaching resources, and host cultural events.

PROJECT TELL. Project Tell was a three-year, $3 million project that focused on assessing the impact of telecommunications technology on children considered to be "at risk." Three initiatives were introduced into nine schools in New York City. PCs in the classroom, PCs in student homes, and parent-teacher communication via voice messaging. City University of New York (CUNY), which was hired to evaluate the effect on the children involved, reported positive results, including decreased dropout rates. The project concluded in 1993.

BUNKER HILL COMMUNITY COLLEGE. A six-site, multichannel analog video network links the college and the Massachusetts Consortium for Education and Technology (MCET) with several Boston high schools. Classes are taught via distance learning from college to local high schools and to classes in other parts of the country.

MEMBERS OF THE SOCIETAL GOALS WORKING GROUP

Marvin Bailey
Ameritech

Ludina Barzini
Rizzoli Carriere della Sera

Glenn Brown
US West

Alan Daley
Bell Atlantic

Laura Ford
US West

Henry Geller
The Markle Foundation

Ken Gordon
Massachusetts Dept of Public
  Utilities

Frank Gumper
NYNEX

Reed Hundt
Federal Communications
  Commission

Julia Johnson
Florida Public Service
  Commission

Patricia Koch
Bell Atlantic

Karen Kornbluh
Federal Communications
  Commission

Joel Lubin
AT&T

Barbara O'Connor
California State University

Robert Sachs
Continental Cablevision

Lawrence Strickling
Ameritech

Brenda Trainor
Clark County (Las Vegas),
  Nevada

FOCAS Representatives and Resources

The following is a list of individuals who contributed to the FOCAS project in 1994 and 1995 as representatives of FOCAS members at the summer preparatory sessions and/or follow-up task force meetings, or as expert resources in the areas of education and technology. Job titles and affiliations at the time of attendance at a FOCAS event are listed.

Rosalyn Andrews
Vice President, Marketing
Time Life Education

Marvin E. Bailey
Vice President
State Technology Programs
Ameritech Indiana

Carol Ann Bischoff
Legislative Assistant
Office of Senator Robert Kerrey

James Blake
Vice President
Hubbard Broadcasting, Inc.

Bonnie Bracey
Teacher-in-Residence
Arlington (Virginia) Career Center

David W. Carr
Associate Professor and Chair
Library and Information Studies
  Department
School of Communications,
  Information, and Library Studies
Rutgers University

Cathy Clark
Program Associate
The John and Mary R. Markle
  Foundation

James Ron Cross
Director, Regulatory Policy
Nortel

Dan Daniels
General Manager for Education
  and Entertainment
Prodigy Services

Tony Das
Executive Secretary
Department of Commerce

Robert J. Erickson
Senior Vice President, Finance
  and Administration
Summit Communications

Charles Firestone
Director
Communications and Society
  Program
The Aspen Institute

Ed Fitzsimmons
Special Assistant
Education and Training
Office of Science and Technology
   Policy
Executive Office of the President

Donna Gardner
Region Vice President
The National PTA

Amy K. Garmer
Program Associate
Communications and Society
   Program
The Aspen Institute

Jim Ginsburg
Senior Information Officer
Jones Interactive

Donald Gips
Office of Plans and Policy
Federal Communications
   Commission
Washington, D.C.

Fred Goldberg
Manager, NYCNET
New York City Board of Education

Daniel Goroff
Department of Mathematics
and
The Derek Bok Center for
   Teaching and Learning
Harvard University

Michael D. Greenbaum
General Manager
Communications Line of Business
Prodigy Services

Jenny Grogg
High School Science Teacher
   and Congressional Fellow
Office of Senator Robert Kerrey

Terry Grunwald
NCexChange Project Director
NC Client and Community
   Development Center
Raleigh, North Carolina

Clark Hammelman
Executive Director of Public
   Policy
US West, Inc.

Bonnie Hathaway
Director of Community Relations
Time Warner Cable
Stamford, Connecticut

Nancy Hechinger
Managing Director
Pantecha, Inc.
New York, New York

Kevin Hess
Director
Government and Regulatory
   Affairs
TDS Telecom

Robert A. Kirschner
Vice President of Planning
   and Rural Economic
   Development
TDS Telecom

Gary Knell
Senior Vice President, Corporate
   Affairs
Children's Television Workshop

Frank Knott
President
Vital Resources

Karen Kornbluh
Office of Plans and Policy
Federal Communications
   Commission

Barbara Kurshan
Vice President
Educorp Consultants
   Corporation

Leanna Landsmann
Leanna Landsmann, Inc.

Linda Lehrer
Director of Communications
The Aspen Institute

John Mack
President
Los Angeles Urban League

Martha Matzke
Director of Special Projects
Office of the President
American Federation of
   Teachers

Jennifer McCarthy
Director of Special Projects
The Nathan Cummings
   Foundation

Gail McClure
Vice President, Communications
   and Strategic Planning
W. K. Kellogg Foundation

Bernadette McGuire-Rivera
Associate Administrator
Office of Telecommunications
   and Information Applications
Department of Commerce
Washington, D.C.

Carol Melton
Vice President, Law and Public
   Policy
Time Warner

Steve McNeal
Acting Treasurer
Entergy Corporation

John Morabito
Attorney
Policy and Program Planning
   Division
Federal Communications
   Commission

Barbara Munder
Senior Vice President
McGraw-Hill, Inc.

Paul Myer
Vice President, Public Affairs
Northern Telecom

Walter Oliver
Senior Vice President, Human
   Resource and Administration
Ameritech

Nancy Pelz-Paget
Director
Program on Education for a
   Changing Society
The Aspen Institute
and

Director of Special Projects and
Marketing
Alvin H. Perlmutter, Inc.
New York, New York

Marcia Reecer
Assistant Director
Office of the President
American Federation of
Teachers

A. J. Remsing
Vice President, Strategic
Analysis
Jones International
Englewood, Colorado

Linda Roberts
Special Advisor on Educational
Technology
Department of Education

Elizabeth Rohatyn
Chairman
Teaching Matters, Inc.

Connie Sage
Director of Corporate Commu-
nications
Landmark Communications, Inc.

Janie R. Smith
Director
Office of High School
Instruction and K–12
Curriculum Services
Fairfax County, Virginia Public
Schools

John Taylor
Vice President of Public Affairs
Zenith Electronics Corporation

Rachel B. Tompkins
Associate Provost for Extension
and Economic Development
West Virginia University

Carol A. Twigg
Vice President
Educom
Washington, D.C.

Tom Upchurch
President
Georgia Partnership for
Excellence in Education

Kate Wallace
Bethesda, Maryland

Dennis Walsh
Vice President and Chief
Information Officer
Entergy Corporation

Richard Weisenhoff
Coordinator of Educational
Technologies
Howard County, Maryland
Public Schools

Janice West
Health and Welfare Commissioner
The National PTA
Stone Mountain, Georgia

Lyle Wilcox
Senior Vice President and Provost
Marshall University

Hunter Williams
Senior Manager for Educational
Relations
Discovery Communications, Inc.

Rita Wilson
Senior Vice President
Corporate Communications
Ameritech

Kathryn Wolfe
Vice President, Product Man-
 agement Network Systems
Zenith Electronics Corporation

The Aspen Institute
Communications and Society Program

The overall goal of the Communications and Society Program is to promote integrated, thoughtful, value-based decision making in the communications and information policy fields. In particular, the Program focuses on the implications of communications and information technologies on democratic institutions, individual behavior, instruments of commerce, and community life.

The Program accomplishes this through two main types of activities. First, it brings together representatives of industry, government, the media, the academic world, the non-profit sector, and others for roundtable meetings to assess the impact of modern communications and information systems on the ideas and practices of a democratic society. Second, the Program promotes research and distributes conference reports to leaders in the communications and information fields, and to the public at large.

Topic areas of the Program fall into three categories: the societal impact of the communications and information infrastructures, communications policy making, and communications for global understanding. Within these areas, the Program has chosen to focus with special interest on the issues of telecommunications and education, electronic democracy, media impact, and electronic commerce.

Charles Firestone is Director of the Aspen Institute's Communications and Society Program. Prior to joining the Institute, he was a private communications and entertainment attorney in Los Angeles and an adjunct professor at the UCLA School of Law, where he also directed the Communications Law Program. Firestone worked previously as an attorney at the Federal Communications Commission and as director of litigation for the Citizens Communication Center in Washington, D.C.

81